"Nicky Silver's best play since *The Food Chain* . . . Hilariously frank, clear-sighted and compassionate and forgiving . . . Laughter that rises in close and regular waves."

—BEN BRANTLEY, *NEW YORK TIMES*

"*The Lyons* is smart and funny and moving . . . a deeply affecting portrait—entertaining and thought-provoking."

—JESSE OXFELD, *NEW YORK OBSERVER*

"Silver's humor is mordant, dark and rich. He's a writer who knows all too well the unsaid hurt that can infect families."

—JOCELYN NOVECK, *ASSOCIATED PRESS*

"Black comedy perfection! Suffice it to say that while Silver is wary of sentimentality or false reconciliation, he deftly shows the ways in which the remaining three Lyons family members reach out for a human connection. Whether they do this with clumsy earnestness or with unapologetic, selfish pragmatism, the playwright's refusal to judge them helps foster our own understanding of these injured and injurious people."

—DAVID ROONEY, *HOLLYWOOD REPORTER*

"A pleasure to be back in Nicky Silver's whirlpool of emotional hunger, despair and unexpected tenderness."

—LINDA WINER, *NEWSDAY*

"Death looms large in Nicky Silver's Broadway play, *The Lyons*, a caustic and canny comedy about family dysfunction packed with surprises that are alternately hilarious, tragic and absurd."

—JOE DZIEMIANOWICZ, *DAILY NEWS*

THE LYONS

BOOKS BY NICKY SILVER AVAILABLE FROM TCG

Etiquette and Vitriol: The Food Chain and Other Plays
INCLUDES:
The Food Chain
Pterodactyls
Fat Men in Skirts
Free Will & Wanton Lust

The Lyons

Raised in Captivity

THE LYONS

Nicky Silver

THEATRE COMMUNICATIONS GROUP
NEW YORK
2012

The Lyons is published by Theatre Communications Group, Inc., 520 Eighth Avenue, 24th Floor, New York, NY 10018-4156

The publication of *The Lyons* by Nicky Silver, through TCG's Book Program, is made possible in part by the New York State Council on the Arts with the support of Governor Andrew Cuomo and the New York State Legislature.

TCG books are exclusively distributed to the book trade by Consortium Book Sales and Distribution.

LIBRARY OF CONGRESS CATALOGING-IN-PUBLICATION DATA

Silver, Nicky.
The Lyons / Nicky Silver. — First Edition.
pages cm
ISBN 978-1-55936-436-2 (trade paper)
ISBN (invalid) 978-1-55936-726-4 (ebook)
I. Title.
PS3569.I4712M35   1999
812'.54—dc23   2012040152

Book design and composition by Lisa Govan
Cover design by Chip Kidd
Cover photograph: Mr. and Mrs. Jerry Silver, circa 1963.

First Edition, December 2012

The Lyons is dedicated to Jerry Silver
1930–2010

Introduction

As I write this we have just begun previews for the Broadway production of *The Lyons*. Today, of course, I have no idea if we'll close on opening night or run for years. (Chances are it'll be somewhere in between.) But at the moment, I find myself on Broadway, a place I never thought I'd be. Now, for those non–New Yorkers, Broadway is a street, a specific place. But in the theater, Broadway is a district, a clump of theaters distinguished by their size—and their place in history. The Cort Theatre, our home, is actually on Forty-eighth Street, east of Seventh Avenue. But it's Broadway just the same.

Given this turn of events, I have been asked lately what it means to me to have a play on Broadway. I respond, "I'm not stupid enough to think that it is some clear indication of quality. Quality is everywhere. But being on Broadway changes, if not how I see myself, at least how others see me. It assures one a place at some historical, theatrical dinner table." (Although given my nature, I suspect I'll be seated in the back, next to the kitchen.) In any event, never having dared to dream this dream, it's actually more moving to me than I can say. It's a shock, frankly. And both of my fans are dumbstruck.

A little background. When I came to New York, in the mid-seventies, all I wanted was to find my place in the theatrical community. I was young, full of rage and that sense of superiority that can only live inside someone who has yet to accomplish a single thing. I thought of Broadway as a pandering, lowbrow circus. Joseph Papp and Stephen Sondheim were exceptions, bringing things like *Runaways* and *Follies* to the Great White Way—but for the most part I was snotty about what was popular. I realize now this is because I wasn't.

I wrote plays that shouted, "Look at me!" *Fat Men in Skirts*, one of my earliest plays to be produced, involves incest and cannibalism (and oddly no chunky transvestites). I still love that play *very* much and it has proven to be very popular both in this country and overseas. But it certainly wasn't the kind of thing that played on Broadway. My point is this: I never thought of myself as one who wrote "Broadway plays." It never occurred to me to even have that dream.

Then, gradually, over the last twenty years two things happened. I changed and Broadway changed. The reasons for the latter are complicated, economic, artistic and better left to someone smarter than I to explain. I changed, well, because I got older. It was inevitable. I suspect I'm still a stretch for some portion of the Broadway audience, but from the first moment of the first preview at the Vineyard Theatre, I sensed this play had a different kind of appeal, an enthusiasm that brought me here.

How on earth did this happen?

The Lyons was written in 2009. My father, by the way, was relatively healthy and vigorous at the time. He passed away between the time I wrote the play and the play's premiere. (I mention this only to stifle those who think *The Lyons* is strictly reportage.) Several theaters with whom I have relationships stepped up and did readings at once. I didn't think the readings went very well—readings are always dodgy propositions—and *everyone* passed. That brings me to the Vineyard.

The Vineyard Theatre has been my home for twenty years now. I have worked on eleven projects and opened eight plays there. A remarkable relationship in this day and age. We've had big successes (*Pterodactyls*, *Raised in Captivity*) and some that didn't turn out so well (I'm not naming them, go look online if you must). But they've stood by me. They are my family and

I love them deeply. I cannot name them all here, but I have to mention the great Doug Aibel, Jen Garvey-Blackwell, Sarah Stern, Rebecca Habel . . . there are too many. And not just the staff, but the audience, the Vineyard subscribers. They've stood by me, too. I am, it seems, the luckiest playwright in New York.

In any event, the Vineyard was more interested in *another* new play I had just finished. It took a few readings and some gentle arm-twisting to get them to do *The Lyons* instead. That may be overstating it. They always believed in the play, but the readings went a long way toward convincing them that it should go first. One of the problems with the previous readings, one of the reasons they didn't work for me, was casting. I wasn't taking any chances at the Vineyard. The first person I asked for was Michael Esper, to play Curtis.

Michael Esper is my closest friend. He also happens to be the finest actor I know. I didn't write Curtis for Michael, but I knew he would make Curtis work. He brings depth to writing that has none and heart to ice cold words. He did that, from day one, at the first reading. He gave my play a soul. I love him and owe him so, so much.

The readings went well and the Vineyard committed. The next question was Rita. The first person we went to was Linda Lavin. Now Miss Lavin is a Broadway legend with too many awards to list. She is magnificent. I'd never met her and never thought she'd do it. She had offers at the time for two very prestigious Broadway shows! But, what the hell, we sent her the script . . . and she said yes! Working with Miss Lavin, getting to know her, has been one of the great bonuses of *The Lyons*. She leaves the legend outside and brings the hilarious, warm, self-deprecating Linda into rehearsal. And in front of an audience there is simply no one more alive, or brilliantly funny and heart-breaking. Her relationship with the audience is a tangible thing. You can see it in the air. She is a marvel.

The rest of the cast was of equal stature. I'd worked with Dick Latessa, another Tony winner, years ago. I adored him then, adore him now. He marries real gravitas with the humor of a brilliant comic. The stunning Kate Jennings Grant completed the family as Lisa. I'd been a huge fan of Kate's since I saw her in *The Marriage of Bette and Boo*, and I was thrilled to get her! It's rare to find someone that beautiful *and* that gifted. Add Gregory Wooddell and Brenda Pressely as the nonfamily members, and let's face it, with this cast the play would have to stink out loud not to do well. Six spectacular actors. I just got lucky and that's all there is to it.

Now, I must talk about Mark Brokaw, the director of *The Lyons*. We'd worked together briefly, seventeen years ago, and I didn't really know him anymore. We asked him. He read it. And he said yes. Mark is a rock. Putting up a new play is a terrifying thing! Mark always made me feel protected. He's also, thank heavens, completely brilliant. He allows the play and the performances to grow, to blossom, knowing just how much to do and how much room to give. Most directors think they have to yank the play out like a rotten tooth. Mark is gentle and astute and nurturing. He did a *perfect* job.

So we opened at the Vineyard. Reviews were great, really great, and we broke a lot of records. Anyone who writes plays, and continues to write over a span of years, knows that every career has its ups and downs. And, to be honest, the response to *The Lyons* at the Vineyard was more than I'd hoped for. It was thrilling. Right away people started talking about a Broadway transfer. There was talk of that for *Raised in Captivity* [1995] and it didn't happen. So this time I tried not to think about it.

Then, at the eleventh hour, in a wildly busy season, the pieces fell into place. Kathleen K. Johnson stepped up to the plate and offered to move the show. A single name above the title—a rare thing in this day and age, and sign of real faith and real courage.

So here I am. I find myself writing the introduction to this volume during Broadway previews. Whoda thunk it? If we run for days or if we run for years, the ride is the prize. And that's the fact.

There are other people to thank who went on this journey. My great agent John Buzzetti; Terry Kinney; Manny, Jeff and Jason at Niko Companies; Roy and Denise; Sam; the wonderful Penny Fuller . . . so many, too many.

But now I have to get to the theater for tonight's preview and my stomach hurts already.

You see, I get horribly nervous *every* night, every show. Will they laugh tonight? Will they be moved tonight?

Somehow or other, they always laugh.

They're always moved.

Wonders never cease.

Nicky Silver
New York City
April 8, 2012

THE LYONS

PRODUCTION HISTORY

The Lyons received its world premiere at the Vineyard Theatre
(Douglas Aibel, Artistic Director; Sarah Stern, Co-Artistic Director; Jennifer Garvey-Blackwell, Executive Producer; Rebecca
Habel, Managing Director) in New York City on October 11,
2011. It was directed by Mark Brokaw. The set design was by
Allen Moyer, the costume design was by Michael Krass, the light-
ing design was by David Lander and the original music and
sound design were by David Van Tieghem; the production stage
manager was Roy Harris. The cast was:

BEN	Dick Latessa
RITA	Linda Lavin
LISA	Kate Jennings Grant
CURTIS	Michael Esper
A NURSE	Brenda Pressley
BRIAN	Gregory Wooddell

The Lyons subsequently opened on Broadway at the Cort Theatre on April 23, 2012. It was produced by Kathleen K. Johnson.
The cast and all personnel remained the same with the following exceptions: the general manager was Niko Companies, the
production stage manager was Robert Bennett and the stage
manager was Lois Griffing.

CHARACTERS

BEN LYONS: a dying man, although he is at the end of his life, he is not without energy, late seventies

RITA: his wife, sixties to seventies

LISA: their daughter, late thirties

CURTIS: their son, thirties

A NURSE: forties

BRIAN: a very attractive real-estate broker, late twenties to early thirties

TIME AND PLACE

ACT ONE

The Lyons
One evening in a Manhattan hospital room

ACT TWO

Scene 1: Location, Location, Location
One week later, a vacant studio apartment

Scene 2: Most Poor Sons of Bitches
Three days later, a hospital room

Act One

THE LYONS

A hospital room, the bed and two chairs. Ben Lyons, a curmudgeon, is in bed, attached to a drip and perhaps a monitor. A vast array of medication sits on the table next to the bed. There are some "get well" cards and the remnants of an assorted box of chocolates on the windowsill. Ben is watching as the Nurse makes a notation on his chart. Rita, Ben's wife, is seated in a chair, looking through an issue of House Beautiful. *Rita turns a page in her magazine.*

RITA: Look at that.
BEN: What?
RITA: What?
BEN: What'd you say?
RITA: I thought you were sleeping.
BEN: What'd you say?

(The Nurse exits.)

RITA: I said look at that.
BEN: Look at what?
RITA: I'm trying to get ideas—for the living room.

BEN: I like the living room.

RITA: Yes, I know, dear, but I don't. I hate it. I've always hated it.

BEN *(Under his breath)*: Christ.

RITA: I'm trying to remember where I saw it. This room. The most *beautiful* room. Maybe a magazine. Pale blue walls. Icy blue. Glacier blue. *Stunning.* And a sofa—the *exact* same color in a silk moiré—but the same cold blue, like icicles, so it almost disappears into the wall. Gorgeous! It wasn't a magazine. I saw it, I think. I think I saw it. I mean in person—Bunny Barsch! Remember Bunny Barsch? She always had fantastic taste, beautiful taste, elegant taste. Like goyim. Of course that was years ago, then she had that accident and she was never quite the same. I don't even know where she lives now. Frieda Bronstein told me she was *arrested.* Can you believe that? For shoplifting. *Lipsticks* of all things. I suppose you never really know what people are like, behind closed doors. Then you find out one day. You look back and you realize and lots of things make perfect sense. For instance whatever happened to that Limoges I lent her? Service for twelve with a soup tureen and a matching ladle and a gravy boat with a scroll pattern—

BEN: *What the fuck are you talking about!!?*

RITA: Is filthy language really called for?

BEN: Dear fucking god.

RITA: You know I don't like it. You never used to curse. You used to just shoot icy glares. Now every other word out of your mouth is shit and fuck and cocksucker. I don't think it's becoming.

BEN: Go fuck yourself.

RITA: There. You see? You see? It's as if you're incapable of having a decent conversation.

BEN: I'm not.

RITA: When did you get to be so vulgar?

BEN: My head hurts.

RITA: I'm sure if they thought you needed more pain medication they'd give it to you. Isn't that what that drip is? Isn't that what it's for? You don't want to get addicted.

BEN: Why not? What's the difference?

RITA: Well . . . I don't know but it doesn't seem like a very good idea. Do you want to look at pictures for the living room?

BEN: I like the living room.

RITA: I know, dear. You said that. But everything is so threadbare. And I *never* liked it. Not really. And you never let me buy anything really nice. Money, money, money.

BEN: It's comfortable.

RITA: What would you think of a Marrakech theme? You know, Middle Eastern.

BEN: I'm getting a headache.

RITA: I mean, I realize you won't actually *be there* to enjoy it, but I'd like to think you'd like it.

BEN: I wouldn't.

RITA: Try to keep an open mind. Burnt desert colors, pointed arches, mosaics on the floor.

BEN: I don't care.

RITA: It'd be sweet. Think Bedouin.

BEN: Who gives a shit.

RITA: You could feign interest to be polite.

BEN: I don't want to. Why should I?

RITA: Is it so much to ask? To pretend that you care? I have been saddled with the same living room furniture for thirty years. All mismatched and grotesque. Every stain on every piece of fabric, a reminder of some horrible thing, some disastrous day that I had to live through. Is it too much to want a fresh start? Is it too much to hope for a clean palate. I look at the sofa. I know it was cream when we bought it. Now it's just some washed-out shade of dashed hopes. The chairs are the color of disgust. And the carpet is matted down with resignation.

BEN: What the hell does that mean?

RITA: Is it wrong of me to want a new beginning? I'm not that old. I'm not so old that I should just give up. People who quit are quitters and people who fight are fighters—well, that's sort of obvious, isn't it? I don't want to just dry up and crumble away. Now, you can participate or you can just complain.

(She returns to her magazine. Beat.)

BEN: I'm dying, Rita.

RITA: Yes, I know. But try to be positive. My mother used to say, "Dying's not so bad. Not when you consider the alternative." Was that it? Is that what she said? Maybe it was the other way around.

BEN: I'm scared.

RITA: Of what? Jews don't believe in hell.

BEN: Some do.

RITA: We don't.

BEN: You mean *you* don't.

RITA: You mean you do? You believe in hell?

BEN: I don't know.

RITA: Well, even if there is a hell, I can't believe you're going. I mean it's a little grandiose of you, don't you think, to think you're going to hell? Who are you to get into hell? What have you ever done? Were you nice? No. But so what? Who's nice? And isn't hell really for people like Hitler and Pol Pot? You're just a little man with little sins, if you believe in sin. Try not to think about it. What do you think of Chinese Modern? Everything low, low to the ground. Eating on pillows and sleeping on mats. Or the other way around. Do you think you'd like that?

BEN: No!

RITA: Fine.

(She closes the magazine. Beat.)

Do you want to play cards?

BEN: No.

RITA: Do you want to watch TV?

BEN: No.

RITA: You want to stare blankly into space?

BEN: Are the kids coming?

RITA: Lisa's on her way. I told her to call Curtis.

BEN: Oh god, does he have to come!?

RITA: What do you mean?

BEN: I don't like him.

RITA: That's a terrible thing to say.

BEN: He's creepy.

RITA: He's your son!

BEN: He doesn't like me.

RITA *(Dismissive)*: Well.

BEN: He's so "affected."

RITA: By what? What do you mean?

BEN: And what kind of name is Curtis anyway? I named him Hilly, after my father.

RITA: No one thought that was a good idea.

BEN: He was a good man. My father was a good man.

RITA: Didn't he sell Zyklon B to the Nazis during World War Two?

BEN: He sold *sweaters*.

RITA: I remember it differently.

BEN: They never proved anything! Not a goddamn thing! He was kind and caring and firm. And he could fish.

RITA: So?

BEN: He was an athlete.

(She returns to her magazine.)

RITA: So the man could fish. Isn't that something.

BEN: Everyone liked him. He was a man's man.

RITA: I don't even know what that means. What does that mean? It sounds homosexual.

BEN: It's the opposite. It's someone very manly.

RITA *(Regarding the magazine)*: French Provincial?

BEN: He would've hated Curtis.

RITA: Because he doesn't fish?

BEN: Because he's homosexual.

RITA: You see? You see there? Curtis is a man's man. I mean in the actual, literal meaning of the word.

BEN: I think about him a lot. I think about him all the time.

RITA: Curtis? I thought he never crossed your mind.

BEN: My father.

RITA: Oh.

BEN: I still miss him. He's been gone all these years and I can still hear his voice and smell his odor.

RITA: He had an odor?

BEN: A scent.

RITA: You said odor. You mean like BO? Like body odor?

BEN: Like hard work. Like the outdoors.

RITA: I don't remember that.

BEN: You barely knew him.

RITA: I'd remember if he smelled funny.

BEN: He didn't smell funny.

RITA: All right then, if he smelled bad.

BEN: Stop saying that!

RITA: You brought it up. It's your theory. Your father smelled. You said it.

BEN: Oh, shut the fuck up.

RITA: I never said he smelled. You did!

BEN: He didn't smell! I mean he smelled like himself. Everyone smells. Everyone smells like who they are. I smell. You smell. Everyone smells like something!

RITA: Fine.

BEN: You're just trying to get under my skin. I can't walk out of the room so you have me where you want me. I'm trapped. I have to lie here and listen to you. You knew what I meant. You knew what I meant all along. My father was a great man, a giant man, and you just want to tear him down. You want to degrade him and I have to lie here while you go on and on!

RITA: You're very crabby.

BEN: Fuck you!

RITA: This cancer eating away at you, has put you in a terrible mood, a foul humor.

BEN: You think!? You think so? I can't believe you don't have a degree in psychology with that kind of breathtaking insight! You're a genius, that's what you are, Rita. A fucking, psychological genius!

(She looks at her magazine.)

RITA: What do you think of Early American?

BEN: I forbid you to redecorate my house!

RITA: You forbid me?

BEN: You heard me.

RITA: You have nothing to say about it.

BEN: It's my house! I want it to stay the way it is!!

RITA: Maybe I should get the nurse.

BEN *(Furious)*: Fuck the nurse! And fuck you! I don't want you touching my house! I love the house! I love the living room. I love everything in it!

RITA: Really?

BEN: Except for the people! And it's going to stay the way it is. Forever! You understand me? When they build a highway they can build around it. I don't give a shit! I want to add it to my will. I want it in writing. The sofa stays! The chairs stay! You're so goddamn eager to forget, that you can't wait, you can't even wait until I'm gone to get rid of everything. I made those stains! My ass put the dents in those cushions! They're my dents! You want to forget me as fast as you can, well I don't want it! I don't want it and I won't have it! Do you understand me!

RITA: You have nothing to say about it.

BEN: *I think I do!!*

(Lisa appears in the doorway, unnoticed by Ben and Rita. She's carrying a very sweet, very small plant.)

RITA: It can't be good for you to shout.

BEN: I want to shout! I can do what I want! I've been wanting to shout *every* fucking day of my goddamn life for years!

RITA: You've been shouting for years.

BEN: *Don't change the house!!*

LISA: Hello, Daddy.

RITA: Lisa!

BEN *(To himself)*: Shit.

LISA: I would have been here sooner, but traffic was terrible and I couldn't find parking.

BEN: There's a lot! There's a parking lot!

LISA: I didn't notice.

BEN: It's right there!

RITA: Your father's a little worked up right now.

LISA: I can see that.

BEN *(Worked up)*: I am not "worked up."

RITA: It'll pass.

LISA *(Attempting cheery)*: I brought a plant.

RITA: Very nice. Isn't it nice, Ben? It's a nice plant. Adorable!

BEN: Thank you, pumpkin.

RITA: We'll put it right here. *(She puts the plant by the window)*

BEN: The Bronsteins sent candy.

LISA: Oh?

BEN: Your mother ate it all.

RITA: You ate some.

BEN: One piece.

RITA: You didn't like it.

BEN *(Pouting)*: I got a jelly.

RITA *(To Lisa)*: Where are the boys?

LISA: Chad's with his father—Jeremy's with the sitter.

RITA: At his age?

LISA: He likes her.

BEN: Thanks for the plant.

LISA: I didn't think they should come.

RITA: Have you had him tested?

LISA: Who?

RITA: Jeremy.

LISA: For what?

RITA: You know.

LISA: No, I don't. What do you mean, tested? Tested for what?

RITA *(Bright)*: Nothing, dear. Forget it. I like your shoes. Are they new? They're very smart. They make your feet look itty-bitty.

BEN: Let me look at you.

LISA: Tested how? What do you mean? Tested for what?

RITA: Well dear, it's just that he seems, to me, to be just a little bit retarded.

LISA: What?!

RITA: Not excessively!

LISA: Jeremy?!

RITA: Moderately. Just moderately. A little.

LISA: Why would you say that?

RITA: It's not a criticism.

LISA: Jeremy is not retarded!

RITA: Well, you don't know for sure if you haven't had him tested.

LISA: I would know if my son were retarded.

BEN: You never know.

LISA: They test that sort of thing, at school. —Why would you say that?!

RITA: I didn't mean to upset you.

LISA: How else could I react? What did you expect?

RITA: Honestly, I didn't think about it.

LISA: Do you think *Chad* is retarded?

RITA *(After a quick internal debate)*: No.

LISA: But you think Jeremy—

RITA: Let's not talk about it. Forget I mentioned it. Let's talk about something else.

LISA: I have to call my sponsor.

RITA: You just got here.

BEN: Can't it wait?

LISA *(Looking around)*: . . . Fine. I guess it's fine.

RITA: Good.

LISA: There's no liquor in the room, is there?

RITA: I don't think so.

LISA: How long have you thought my son is retarded?

RITA: Please. Forget I said anything. Just put it out of your mind. Let's have a visit. A nice visit. All right?

(Lisa sits. There's a pause.)

LISA: You look well, Daddy.

RITA: Doesn't he?

BEN: I feel like shit, like a piece of fucking shit that got run over by a truck.

RITA *(Confidentially)*: He curses a lot now.

BEN: I can hear you, motherfucker!

LISA: You know, um, you didn't say much. When you called. I mean you said that Dad has cancer, but you didn't say—

BEN: I do. That's right. I have cancer.

LISA: Yes. But I mean—what *kind* of cancer?

RITA: What kind?

LISA: That's right, what kind? Where is it?

RITA: Where isn't it? It started in his kidney, they think, but now it's everywhere. It's in his bones, his colon, his lungs, his asparagus—

LISA: His what?

RITA: Did I say asparagus? I meant esophagus, or appendix. Do you still have your appendix?

BEN: I dunno.

RITA: It's taken hold.

LISA: Oh my god.

RITA: It's *everywhere.*

LISA: I didn't— How do you feel?

BEN: How do you think?

LISA: So this is serious. This is— When did you find out?

BEN: A few months ago

RITA: He never sees doctors. He says he's too busy. Busy with what? That's what I want to know. He hasn't worked since god knows when. He just sits around the house and—

LISA: Wait, wait. Just wait. You've known this *for months?*

BEN *(To Rita):* I do things!

RITA: A few months.

LISA: Why didn't you tell me?

RITA: I meant to dear, but frankly, I got busy.

BEN *(Disdainful):* She plays backgammon now.

RITA: I was in a tournament!

LISA: So you forgot to tell me that my father is sick?!

BEN: By the time we found out there was nothing to do.

RITA: A fait accompli.

BEN: It's inside me and it's alive.

RITA: So really. Why burden you? You have your own problems.

LISA: You're my parents!

BEN: Your hands are full.

RITA: You have the boys.

BEN: All by yourself.

RITA: Are you seeing anyone?

BEN: Why trouble you.

RITA: We decided not to tell you, or Curtis—until the end.

LISA: . . . The end?

BEN: That's right. The end . . . I'm dying.

(There's a long pause while Lisa tries to process this.)

LISA: You're dying.

BEN: Yes.

LISA: I didn't, I don't, um—I don't—

RITA: Are you all right?

BEN: It's any time now.

LISA: You should have told me. You should have. I could've been prepared.

RITA: I thought I made it clear.

LISA *(Snapping)*: You didn't.

RITA: I'm sorry.

LISA *(To Ben)*: It's just— You don't look like you're dying.

BEN: Looks are deceiving.

LISA: This isn't happening. It can't be. Have you seen doctors—I mean a second opinion?

BEN: And a third.

RITA: We've had time to adjust.

(Lisa takes a moment and really processes this.)

LISA *(Fragile)*: . . . You're dying.

(Ben nods.)

RITA: And we thought, now that it's, well, imminent, we thought you should be here.

LISA: I see.

RITA: It's all right. It is. We're ready. He's ready. Your father's had a good life.

BEN: Not really.

RITA: What do you mean by that?

BEN: What could I mean by "not really"?

RITA: He's had a good life. By most people's standards. He's a very half-glass-empty kind of person, but by most people's standards he's had a very full life.

BEN: Says you.

RITA: But now, well . . . we thought you should be here.

LISA: Of course.

RITA: To say anything that you might want to say.

LISA: Oh.

RITA: Before it's too late.

LISA: I see.

(Beat.)

RITA: Is there something?

LISA: What?

RITA: That you want to say?

LISA: Oh. Now? You mean, now?

RITA *(Confidential)*: I wouldn't wait.

LISA: Oh.

RITA: Whatever you like. A poem. Or you might want to share a memory, if you can put your finger on something pleasant. Or just talk about your feelings, whatever they are. You know, something meaningful.

LISA: Of course. Yes. Of course, I'd like to.

RITA: Well?

(Lisa stands by the bed.)

LISA: Daddy, I um . . . I . . . well . . .

(A long pause while Lisa tries to think of something meaningful to say.)

RITA: No pressure, dear.

LISA *(Snapping at her)*: Let me think!

RITA: Sorry.

(They watch while Lisa strains to remember something. Lisa's quite emotional when she finally speaks.)

LISA: Daddy . . . I remember . . . when I was little, six or seven maybe, and I was playing on the jungle gym and you were watching, and you looked away for just a second, and I fell and—oh, shit. That's a movie.

RITA: *Kramer vs. Kramer!*

BEN: I'm getting sleepy.

RITA: I loved that picture!

LISA: It'll come to me! Something will come. It's a lot to process!

RITA: Don't worry about it. Please. Something will pop into your head, I'm sure. Like when you're trying to remember someone's name. You try and try and come up empty. And then all of a sudden—there it is!

LISA: I give up.

RITA: Good.

BEN: Well, that was a bust.

RITA *(To Lisa)*: I wish you'd brought candy or something. I'm starving. And I have a terrible taste in my mouth.

LISA: I could go downstairs?

RITA: No, no. It's fine.

LISA: There might be something in my purse.

(Lisa looks through her purse.)

RITA: Did you call your brother?

LISA: Yes.

RITA: Good.

LISA: A piece of licorice!

RITA: Red?

LISA: Black.

RITA: Forget it.

BEN: I was sure you'd have *something* to say. Not Curtis maybe, but you. I would've bet on it.

LISA: I could try again?

RITA: Please don't. It was embarrassing.

LISA *(Defeated)*: Fine.

(Beat.)

RITA: Listen. I was thinking, what if you and the boys come and visit, stay with me—for a little while.

LISA: Why?

RITA: To keep me company.

LISA *(Skeptical)*: Really?

BEN: You don't have to.

RITA: Maybe she wants to.

LISA: The boys have school.

RITA: We can homeschool them!

BEN: That's for crackpots.

RITA: That's not true. Many wonderful people have been home-schooled. All kinds of people. Presidents and captains of industry.

BEN: Name two.

RITA: Right now?

BEN: Crackpots. Crackpots and religious fanatics.

RITA: Please. You're the one who's all of a sudden afraid of hell.

BEN: Leave the boys where they are. You don't want them. You don't really like them anyway.

RITA: That's not true!

LISA: You don't like your grandchildren?

RITA: I adore them.

BEN: She doesn't.

LISA: Why don't you like them?

RITA: I do! I mean, Chad takes after his father a little too much, and Jeremy, as I said, I think is slightly retarded. But I like them! Of course, I like them. They're my grandchildren!

BEN: She's full of crap.

RITA: You should come for a visit, a long visit. We'll have fun!

LISA: Well, I'll think about it.

BEN: That means no.

LISA: Do we have to decide this minute?

RITA: Certainly not. Do you want to look at some decorating magazines? I'm redoing the living room.

LISA: Oh, thank god. It's awful.

BEN: It is not.

LISA: Daddy, please.

BEN: I like it.

LISA: It's disgusting. You walk into the house and you think, "My god, poor people live here." You live like poor people. Is that what you want people to think?

BEN: Who gives a fuck what people think?

(Lisa joins Rita. They look at a magazine together.)

RITA: I'm seeing pale blue walls. Icy blue.

BEN: You care too much what people think.

RITA: Glacial blue.

LISA: It sounds a little cold.

RITA: That's what I'm going for.

BEN: Do you hear from David?

LISA: I see him when he sees the boys.

RITA: Oh, good.

BEN: You should move, You should move out of the state, That'd teach him, the motherfucker.

RITA *(Regarding the cursing)*: You hear that?

BEN: It's his fault. I never liked him. Selfish, juvenile bastard. It's *all* his fault.

LISA: What are you talking about? What's his fault?

BEN: Your drinking. It's his fault you started drinking. You never drank before the two of you got married. Never! Not a cocktail, a glass of wine at dinner—nothing! He started you. He started you and look what happened. He's to blame!

LISA: We met at Alcoholics Anonymous!!

BEN: I blame him!

RITA *(Regarding the magazine)*: Do you think plaid is too casual?

(Curtis appears in the doorway. He's holding a plant that is several times larger than the one Lisa brought. It is so large, in fact, that his head can't quite be seen over the top of it.)

CURTIS: Hello?

RITA: Curtis!

CURTIS: How is everyone?

RITA: Let me take that.

CURTIS: Thank you.

RITA *(Taking the plant)*: So heavy!

CURTIS: Can you manage?

(Rita puts the large plant next to the very small plant Lisa brought. Beat. They all look at them for a moment.)

LISA: Well. He's not raising two children all by himself!

CURTIS: What, is David on the dole or something?

LISA: "On the dole"? What are you British now?

CURTIS: Don't you get child support?

LISA: Oh, shut up.

RITA: You look wonderful.

CURTIS: Thank you.

RITA: How's your weight?

CURTIS: You're looking right at me.

RITA: Who can tell?

(Curtis takes off his jacket and puts it on a chair.)

CURTIS: How are you, Dad? How are you feeling?

LISA: He's dying.

CURTIS: What?

LISA: He's dying.

CURTIS: Oh for god's sake Lisa, everything with you is tragedy.

LISA: You don't understand—

CURTIS: I mean, we're all dying, aren't we?

LISA: Not this week, we're not!

CURTIS: What?

LISA: He's dying.

CURTIS: . . . What do you mean?

LISA: He has cancer, apparently in every inch of him, and he's going to die—tonight, tomorrow, maybe next week.

BEN: Not next week.

CURTIS: Oh my god.

RITA: It's true.

CURTIS: Oh my god.

LISA: That's right. And they've known this. They've known about this for some time, the two of them, *and they never told us.*

CURTIS: You're dying?

LISA: Did you hear me? They've known this for months. They never said a thing!

RITA: We didn't want to bother you.

LISA: Can you believe that! Our father is clinging to life by a cobweb—and they never mentioned it!

CURTIS: Well . . . Actually, I think that's nice. I think it's sort of considerate.

LISA: What!?

CURTIS: I think it's thoughtful.

LISA: You're serious?

CURTIS: In fact, given the grotesquely narcissistic and infantile standard by which they normally operate, I think it's surprisingly generous.

RITA: Thank you, dear.

LISA: It's insane! It's insane and selfish! That's what it is. And the fact that you don't really care is just indicative of how little you care about anything or anyone for that matter!

RITA: Please! Let's not argue. We're never together, all four of us. Let's talk about something pleasant.

(There's a long, awkward pause. They all just look at each other.)

CURTIS: Does it hurt?

BEN: I'm on a drip.

(Another awkward pause.)

RITA: Is Peter coming?

CURTIS *(Shaking his head)*: Oral surgery.

RITA: Oh.

CURTIS: Sorry.

RITA: He must have terrible teeth.

CURTIS: Not really.

RITA: He always seems to have—

CURTIS: Bad gums.

(Yet another awkward pause.)

RITA: Are you writing anything? Are you working on anything?

CURTIS: Not right now.

LISA: I have to say, I think it's in terrible taste, I do, to show up at a hospital *with a potted tree.*

CURTIS: You *have* to say that?

LISA: Yes. That's right. I have to.

RITA: We were lucky to get this private room.

BEN: They put me in semi-private first. The other guy had a baboon heart.

RITA: He did not.

BEN: You don't listen.

RITA: He was here for gallstones.

BEN: Fuck you!

RITA: Your father feels that imminent death gives him license to—

BEN: Talk the way I want? You bet your fat ass.

CURTIS: Good for you.

BEN: Go fuck yourself!

CURTIS (*To Lisa*): How long are visiting hours?

LISA (*Despairing*): I have no idea.

RITA (*Bright, to Curtis*): You know what I was thinking? Maybe you'd like to come for a visit. Stay with me for a while.

LISA: I thought *I* was coming?

RITA: You said you didn't want to.

LISA: I said I'd think about it.

RITA: Six of one, dear, really.

CURTIS (*To Lisa*): How are the kids?

LISA: They're fine.

CURTIS: Is Jeremy better?

LISA: He is not retarded!

CURTIS: You had him tested?

LISA: Let's watch TV.

(*Lisa looks for the remote. The phone rings. Rita goes to it.*)

BEN: God, I hope it's death.

LISA: That's not funny, Daddy. It's just in bad taste.

RITA (*Into the phone*): Hello?

LISA (*To Curtis*): Where did you park?

CURTIS: There's a lot.

BEN: I told you!

RITA (*To Curtis*): It's for you.

CURTIS: That'll be Peter. I told him to call.

(*Curtis takes the phone.*)

BEN (*To Rita*): The man had a baboon heart.

RITA: That was a movie. You're confused.

CURTIS (*Into the phone*): I'm okay.

RITA (*To Lisa*): He gets confused.

BEN: I do not.

CURTIS (*Into the phone*): I don't know.

RITA: Last night he thought I was Suzanne Pleshette.

BEN: I said I *wished* you were Suzanne Pleshette.

RITA *(To Lisa)*: It's the drugs.

CURTIS *(Into the phone)*: Not too late . . . I love you, too.

(Curtis hangs up.)

RITA: How's his mouth?

CURTIS: His what?

RITA: His gums.

CURTIS: Oh, fine.

RITA *(To Lisa)*: When are *you* going to find someone?

LISA: Oh, I dunno. I was going to do it today, but then you called and here I am.

RITA: What happened to that Bill?

LISA: You mean Bob?

RITA: He was darling. He was so attractive, all that beautiful hair. And he had very good manners. He always called me "Mrs. Lyons" no matter how many times I told him to call me "Rita," he insisted. And I liked his hands and he had very broad—

LISA: He had herpes. All right?

RITA: Oh . . . Well. I see. Herpes. Hmmm.

CURTIS: So, he had herpes? So what? If you cared about him, what's the difference? It doesn't kill you.

LISA: I know that.

CURTIS: It shouldn't matter.

LISA: It mattered to me. I couldn't feel . . . comfortable, when we were intimate.

RITA: Really dear, *no one* feels comfortable when they're intimate.

BEN: Your mother used to vomit a lot.

RITA: Don't tell people that!

BEN: It's true.

RITA *(To Lisa)*: I don't understand it. You're a sweet girl. You're perfectly nice looking—

LISA: Thanks so much.

RITA: I mean it. Since you stopped boozing and lost all the weight.

CURTIS *(To himself)*: Unbelievable.

RITA: Maybe you don't like men.

LISA: Maybe they don't like me.

BEN: Maybe she's gay. Like what's-his-name.

CURTIS *(Annoyed)*: My name is Curtis.

BEN: Not really.

LISA: I'm not gay!

RITA: Then I don't understand it. I mean what man in his right mind wouldn't adore you?

CURTIS: Herpes isn't the end of the world.

RITA *(A great idea)*: You know what? There's a very nice young man down the hall, Leonard something, end stages of lymphoma—*and* I think he's Jewish!

LISA: What?

RITA: I've talked to his mother. Lovely. Go meet him.

LISA: I don't think so.

RITA: You don't try! That's why you're alone. Go say hello!

LISA: I don't want to!

BEN: She doesn't want to!

RITA: Is there someone better on the horizon? Is there? Is there some line of suitors I know nothing about? From what I can see you're home, all alone, waiting for some perfect man to knock on your door, out of the blue and that's just not—

LISA: There's David!

(Pause.)

RITA: Your David?

BEN: Are you seeing that cocksucker?

LISA: He's not a cocksucker.

RITA: It's a figure of speech, dear.

CURTIS: She sees him.

LISA *(Defensive)*: When he picks up the boys.

CURTIS: And sometimes—

LISA *(Sharp)*: Stop talking! It's my business.

RITA: Is something there? Is something brewing?

LISA: I don't know.

RITA: I loved you as a couple. David and Lisa. Like that movie. What was that called?

CURTIS: *David and Lisa.*

LISA: I don't know. We're talking. We're just talking. It's good for the boys.

BEN: He started your drinking.

LISA: Oh for god's sake. I was drunk in the fourth grade! I didn't even know him!

RITA: Has he said anything?

LISA: About what?

RITA: Reconciling.

LISA: No.

BEN: Thank god.

RITA: Has he met anyone?

LISA: I don't think so.

RITA: Then it could, it could work out. I think that would be wonderful! Things happen. People go away and they come back. It's not so unusual. Famous people do it all the time. You two could get back together.

CURTIS: What the hell is the matter with you?

RITA: What do you mean?

CURTIS: That's what you want? They should get back together?

LISA: You don't know him!

CURTIS: I know enough.

BEN: What does that mean?

LISA *(To Curtis)*: It's so easy for you.

CURTIS: That you're even considering—

LISA: You weren't there! With us!

CURTIS: He's an asshole.

LISA: He is not!! You don't know him! . . . You don't. He used to look at me. And we just—we communicated something. We connected. He trusted me . . . He looked at me. He thought I could help him. He thought I could save him.

RITA *(Quiet)*: That's a lot.

LISA: I still see him, all the time, brown hair, straight hair, beautiful eyes. Looking at me. At night, the boys are asleep and the room is quiet. I listen for him. Next to me. The sound of breathing . . . It hurts so much.

CURTIS: And?

LISA: And he loved me.

CURTIS: And?

LISA: And I fucked up.

RITA: How?

LISA: He thought I could save him—

CURTIS: And.

LISA: And nothing.

CURTIS: For god's sake.

LISA: And nothing!

CURTIS: Say it.

LISA: You promised me!

CURTIS: Just say it!

LISA: It's private! Do you understand me? It's private!

CURTIS: And he hit you!

BEN: What!

CURTIS: He hit her.

LISA: You promised!

BEN: Motherfucker.

LISA *(To Curtis)*: YOU PROMISED ME!

CURTIS: Not just once.

LISA: Stop it.

CURTIS: All the time.

LISA: It wasn't his fault!

CURTIS *(To Rita)*: Still hope they reconcile?

LISA: It wasn't that bad!

CURTIS: You called me from the hospital!

LISA: One time!

CURTIS *(To Rita)*: You should've seen her.

LISA: It was my fault!

CURTIS: All bloody. Blood everywhere.

LISA: You promised me!! You swore to me! You stood there and you promised that you'd never say it—you'd never tell anyone!

CURTIS: I lied.

LISA: I have to go—

CURTIS: It's fine, if that's what you want—

LISA: I have to call someone.

CURTIS: Let him hit you—

LISA: I have to call my sponsor!

CURTIS: But don't call me when you go over a cliff!

LISA: *YOU DON'T KNOW HIM!! YOU WEREN'T THERE!!*

CURTIS: . . . True. So do what you want. Let him beat the holy fucking crap out of you. It's not my business.

LISA *(Fighting tears, getting her purse)*: I, I—I have to make a call.

RITA *(Offering)*: Use the phone.

LISA: I'll be back. I'll be—I just—I'll be right back. I need some air. Excuse me.

(Lisa exits. Beat.)

RITA *(Quietly)*: I had no idea.

(There's a pause. No one moves. The Nurse enters and looks at Ben's IV drip.)

NURSE: Are you in pain?

BEN: Yes.

(The Nurse adjusts the drip, punching numbers on its keypad.)

NURSE: That should help.

(The Nurse takes Ben's chart from its holder on the wall and makes notes for a moment, then replaces it.)

I'll come back later.

(The Nurse smiles at Rita, then exits.)

RITA *(Quiet)*: I like her.

CURTIS: She seems nice.

BEN: She is.

(Beat.)

RITA: Romance is a treacherous arena.

BEN: What the fuck does that mean?

RITA: I was talking about Lisa.

BEN: Speak English.

RITA: Not everything is about you, you know.

BEN: Could it be? Is that possible? I mean, I am dying.

RITA *(To Curtis)*: You're very lucky. You and Peter. You never fight, do you?

CURTIS: Not much.

RITA: That's very rare.

BEN: It's freakish.

RITA: Your father and I . . . I remember one time, one summer. You were at camp, so you were maybe nine, or twelve. Your father and I were fighting *all* the time. You fight when there are children around, but it's different when they're not. When the kids are at camp the knives come out. It was incredibly hot that summer—we had air-conditioning of course, but still the heat made everyone edgy all the time. You can only smile blankly so many times in response to someone at the hardware store chirping blithely, "Hot enough for you?" . . . That was a terrible summer. Do you remember that, Ben?

BEN: How do I know?

RITA: That hot summer.

BEN: Summers are hot.

RITA: The children were at camp.

BEN: It's always hot in the summer.

RITA: You remember.

BEN: That's why it's summer.

RITA: Think back.

BEN: I might remember! I didn't say I don't. But how the hell do I know if I remember if I don't know what the fuck you're talking about?

RITA: You decided, that summer, while Curtis and Lisa were at camp, that Curtis was a homosexual.

CURTIS: He *decided*?

RITA: He got it into his head.

BEN: I was right, wasn't I?

RITA: That isn't the point.

BEN: I knew it. I knew it before anyone else.

CURTIS: How old am I in this story?

RITA: I'm not sure. Seven—or thirteen.

BEN: I could smell it.

RITA: Ben, please. Enough with the smells. *(To Curtis)* Before you got here he went off on a terrible jag all about how his father had BO and smelled like fish or something.

BEN: He did not have BO!

CURTIS: Grandpa Hilly?

RITA *(To Ben)*: You said it. Not me.

BEN: He was a monumental man. You should be proud to have his name.

CURTIS: I don't think it's even really a name. "Hilly." Wasn't it short for something?

RITA: Nobody knows.

BEN *(To Curtis)*: He would've hated you.

CURTIS: Thanks.

RITA: I was saying. You were at camp, and your father got it into his head that you were queer. Is that an all right word?

CURTIS: It doesn't matter.

BEN: We used "faggot" then. Nobody cared.

RITA: And he decided he had to do something about it.

CURTIS: Like what?

BEN: Electric shock.

CURTIS: You're kidding, right?

BEN: Half.

RITA: He wouldn't talk to anyone about it. He was so embarrassed. I mean the grandson of *Ernest-Hilly-Lyons-Hemmingway* turns out to be some fudge-packing pansy. He was mortified. I loved it. The point is he had to do something and didn't know what. So he sent me to the library, because *he* couldn't check books out about this, not on this subject. So I brought him some books and he read them. Some of them. And he still didn't know what to do. All he could think of was throwing out all your toys—and the *Judy Garland at Carnegie Hall* album.

CURTIS: I can't believe that didn't work.

RITA: I loved that record. When she shouts, "We'll stay all night, we'll sing them all." I still get chills.

BEN: You had other records.

RITA: He replaced it with the *Ballad of the Green Beret*.

CURTIS: I remember that. I came home and all my toys were gone—except the little green army men.

RITA: I was furious. And he wouldn't talk about it. I said to him, "You'd rather he grow up a little green army man, than find someone and fall in love—" And he said, "Obviously." And he slammed a lot of doors and snapped at everyone. It was horrible . . . And that's the time I bought the gun.

BEN: You had a gun?

RITA: That's right.

BEN: Where'd you get a gun?

RITA: Do you remember Victor Cardin, two doors down?

CURTIS: The Cardins. Lawn furniture in their living room?

RITA: Exactly. He repossessed cars. For a living. That's what he did. He found a gun in the back seat of a Cutlass Supreme. He was a nice man.

BEN: You bought a gun?

RITA: Are you not following the story!?

CURTIS: It *is* hard to believe.

RITA: Why?

BEN: What'd you pay for it?

RITA: Seventy-five dollars. He wanted a hundred, but I paid him seventy-five and made him one of those strawberry Jell-O molds with floating bananas.

BEN: What kind of gun?

RITA: I don't know. It had a number. A handgun. Black. It was not without its visual appeal.

CURTIS: You were that upset—because of me?

RITA: Actually, because of the record. Have you ever heard the *Ballad of the Green Beret*? Tuneless. Utterly tuneless. Anyway, I asked Victor Cardin where I could buy bullets and he told me and so the next time I went to get my hair done I made a detour . . . I remember. I was sitting in the kitchen—you were at work—I was sitting at the table, putting the bullets in a gun and hoping I was doing it right. I mean, I'd never held a gun before.

BEN *(Quiet)*: Oh my god.

RITA: I didn't know if I'd be able to use it, to shoot. Or if I would be good at it. I thought I should check. So I went into the backyard, it was very quiet. Middle of the day, on a Tuesday. I lifted the gun. I could hear my own breathing, nothing else. I was very nervous. And I aimed it. I pointed it at the weeping willow next to where the swing set used to be . . . And I shot it . . . It was very loud. It startled me. I dropped the gun and I stood there for a moment and I thought . . . "That's that. That's all you have to do. It's not so hard." . . . And then it occurred to me that I should check, that I should look to see if I had hit what I was aiming at. I went over to the tree, to the weeping willow, and I couldn't find the hole. Then I looked at the swing set . . . Nothing. So then I started at one end of the fence and worked my way, one foot at a time, looking very carefully until I found it. The hole. And by then it was getting late, the sky was turning dark and it was time to start dinner . . . A few days later I sold the gun *back* to Victor Cardin. He'd only give me fifty dollars. But I didn't want it in the house.

(Ben is obviously shaken by her story.)

BEN: You tried to kill me.
RITA: No, no. I shot a hole in a fence.
BEN: You wanted to.
RITA: That's all.
BEN: You wanted to kill me.
RITA: It was a whim.
CURTIS: Why didn't you leave?
RITA: What, dear?
CURTIS: I mean if you were thinking of murder, you could've just left.
RITA *(Realizing this)*: . . . You know that *never* occurred to me.
BEN: My head hurts.
RITA *(Brighter)*: Oh, I'm sorry. Maybe that nurse should come and do whatever she does whenever she comes.
BEN: I think so.
RITA: I'll go look for her.

(She starts to leave.)

You don't happen to know her name, do you?
BEN: No.
RITA: I'll find her. How many nurses can there be? I'll find her.

(Rita exits. There's a pause.)

BEN: Your mother is a bitch.
CURTIS: Apparently.

BEN: She smiles a lot, so she seems nice. And she keeps talking, in that *way*, so that people don't notice. But the truth is, she's a bitch.

CURTIS: Was she always?

BEN: I'm not sure.

CURTIS: Why did you stay?

BEN: With her?

CURTIS: Yes.

BEN *(Simple)*: I loved her.

CURTIS: Oh.

BEN: My fault.

CURTIS: What?

BEN: I still do.

CURTIS: Really?

BEN: Sometimes, I have to remember who she was, but most of the time, who she was is still there. Somewhere. I can still see her when I look at her. Some of the time.

(Beat. Curtis has something difficult to say.)

CURTIS: I want to tell you something.

BEN: I think she was, maybe, always a bitch. I can't remember now.

CURTIS: I want to say something.

BEN: Say it.

CURTIS *(With difficulty)*: . . . I forgive you.

BEN: What?

CURTIS: I forgive you.

BEN: For what?

CURTIS: For making sure I knew, I wasn't the child that you wanted.

BEN *(Still)*: . . . Fuck you.

CURTIS: I wanted to say it.

BEN: I don't need you to forgive me.

CURTIS: I wanted to tell you.

BEN: Who the fuck do you think you are?

CURTIS: Your son.

BEN: I named my son Hilly. After my father.

CURTIS: I know!

BEN: A great man.

CURTIS: I just wanted to say it.

(Beat.)

BEN: Why are you here? We don't see you. You're not part of us. Not really.

CURTIS: I have my life!

BEN: You walk in here and you "forgive me"!? Go fuck yourself.

CURTIS: It would be easy, you know. It would be nothing to kill you. I could take a pillow, I could hold it, press it on to you, until you were dead. And it would be nothing.

BEN: So do it. I'm going to die soon anyway. You think I care how it ends? I don't. My life is one long parade of disappointments. And you're the grand fucking marshal. Do it!

(Lisa appears in the doorway. She is much more relaxed and cheerful than when she left.)

LISA: Let's all go to the maternity ward!

CURTIS: What?

LISA: To see the babies!

CURTIS: Why on earth?

LISA: I was thinking, in the elevator, wouldn't that be fun? It would be fun! We could all go look at babies! *(To Ben)* Well, not you.

CURTIS: Why?

LISA: They're so cute! All pink and fat and squishy with their little fingers and their little feet.

BEN: You go if you want.

LISA: Where's Mother?

BEN: Looking for the nurse.

LISA: I love looking at babies. You know they say that birth is very traumatic. Maybe the most traumatic moment in your whole life. I read that somewhere.

CURTIS: I'm sorry, Lisa.

LISA: Or maybe it was chicks, chickens. You know, chickens— getting out of the egg.

CURTIS: I said I'm sorry.

LISA: For what?

CURTIS: For what I said, for what I did. Before.

LISA: You shouldn't have. It was wrong and I don't know that I forgive you. Chickens! It was chickens. It was absolutely chickens!

CURTIS *(Under his breath)*: Oh Christ.

LISA: What? What? What's the matter?

CURTIS: Have you been drinking?

LISA: Have I been what? Of course not! God! I don't drink. I haven't had a drink in years! Five years, clean and sober! You think I'm an idiot? You think I'm gonna throw that all away? I have children! I have a life! I have made a life for myself. I know I can't drink! I'm not an idiot! How dare you? How dare you stand there on your own two feet and—

CURTIS: You've been drinking.

LISA: A little bit, just a little bit.

CURTIS: Jesus Christ.

LISA: So what!? So I have. I've been drinking. It's my life. And don't stare at me like that. You're not my mother.

BEN: Here we go!

LISA: I won't embarrass you. Don't worry, Daddy. —That's all he cares about.

BEN: Where's the goddamn nurse!?

LISA *(To Curtis)*: He didn't care—he didn't care that I drank. *Nobody* cared! Until I made a spectacle of myself at that god-forsaken country club. Like no one ever got drunk before. Like no one ever made a scene or talked too loud or fought with their husband.

BEN: You urinated on the dance floor!

LISA: *It was an accident!!*

BEN: Well, let's hope.

(Rita enters, holding a box of candy.)

RITA: I couldn't find the nurse. But I did get candy.

LISA: Where'd you get that?

RITA: A little girl down the hall just died. I got Jordan Almonds!

CURTIS: Lisa's drinking.

RITA: What? Really?

LISA: "Lisa's drinking. Lisa's drinking." Why don't you take out a goddamn ad?

(Lisa takes a fifth of whiskey from her purse. She pours it into a cup.)

RITA *(To herself)*: God, you leave the room for a minute.

LISA *(Taking the almonds)*: Gimme those.

RITA: I was so hoping for a pleasant visit.

CURTIS: Yes. Well. Best laid plans and all of that.

RITA: What?

CURTIS: I think I should get going.

RITA: No, no! You can't. We haven't settled when you're coming.

CURTIS: When I'm coming?

RITA: To visit. To stay with me.

LISA: My invitation's apparently expired.

CURTIS: I'm not coming.

RITA: You can help redecorate. We'll have fun! I've been looking at magazines for ideas.

CURTIS: I can't. I'm sorry. I have to think of Peter.

RITA: You can bring him.

CURTIS: He has work. It's not a good time.

RITA: It'll be nice. We could get to know each other.

CURTIS: You and I?

RITA: Peter and I.

CURTIS: I don't think so.

RITA: But—

CURTIS: I'm sorry.

RITA *(Demanding)*: *Why not!?*

CURTIS *(Firm)*: He has things. He has his life. He can't just drop everything, he can't just walk away so we can keep you company. I'll call you later or you call me if anything—

RITA: Are you ashamed of me?

CURTIS: Of course not.

RITA: Well, I think it's very strange. I do. You've been with Peter for three years and we've never met. Do you realize that? I've never laid eyes on this person.

CURTIS: Of course, you have. Last year, at your birthday.

RITA: He didn't come! You said he was sick. I want to know what you're ashamed of.

CURTIS: I'm not ashamed—

RITA: If it's not us, is it him? Is there something about Peter?

CURTIS: Of course not.

RITA: Just tell me!

LISA: He's imaginary.

RITA: I'm talking to your brother!

CURTIS: I have to go.

RITA: I don't understand—

LISA *(Standing)*: You never met him because he doesn't exist!!

RITA: What?

LISA: He made him up.

CURTIS: Shut up, Lisa.

LISA: Tell her. There is no Peter. Go on, tell her. There never was.

RITA: I spoke to him on the phone.

LISA: That was just some friend, or someone he paid—probably a homeless person.

RITA: I spoke to him!

LISA *(Taking Curtis's jacket)*: There is no Peter. And remember Ethan? There was no Ethan.

RITA: Oh my god.

CURTIS: Give me my jacket.

LISA: Imaginary.

CURTIS: Give it to me!

LISA: *All* imaginary.

CURTIS: Lisa—

LISA: Curtis is alone. That's right! He doesn't have anyone. Or see anyone or *touch* anyone—

CURTIS: Stop it!

LISA: And I don't think he ever has. It's all a lie. A giant, fucking, monumental, pathological lie!

RITA *(To Curtis)*: Is that true?

LISA: A fiction!

RITA: Is it true!?

LISA: It's creepy.

CURTIS: I have to go.

RITA: ANSWER ME!

CURTIS: *YES!*

RITA *(Shaken)*: Oh my god.

LISA *(Victorious)*: . . . And *now,* I forgive you.

(He snatches his jacket.)

RITA *(To Curtis)*: Why would you do that?

CURTIS: It was easy. Easier than having you at me.

LISA: Ask him when the last time was.

RITA: The last time for what?

LISA: He's the man in the glass booth.

CURTIS: Fuck you.

LISA: You judge me, but you're just a freak.

RITA: I don't understand.

LISA: There never was a Peter. There never was an Ethan. Although, sometimes, I think, he thought there was.

RITA: I just wanted you to find someone.

LISA: It's pathetic.

RITA: To love someone.

CURTIS: Like you? Who did you love, tell me, ever, in your whole life?

RITA *(Simple)*: You.

(He has no response. He turns to Lisa.)

CURTIS: You are a horrible person. *(To all of them)* You are all horrible people. *I hope I live the rest of my life and never lay eyes on any of you again!!*

(Curtis exits. There's a pause.)

LISA *(Very bright)*: Wow . . . I had forgotten *how much fun* drinking can be.

RITA: That was cruel.

LISA *(Toasting her)*: Well, que—as they say in the song—sera.

(Rita looks at Ben. His eyes are closed and she realizes he hasn't spoken for some time.)

RITA: Find the nurse.

(Lisa rushes out. Rita walks slowly to the window. After a moment the Nurse enters, followed by Lisa. She approaches Ben, and checks his pulse.)

NURSE: Mr. Lyons is sleeping.
RITA: Oh.
NURSE: His breathing is shallow, from the medicine.
RITA: Of course.
NURSE: He should sleep through the night.
RITA: Thank you.

(The Nurse nods and exits. Beat.)

I looked at him, I thought . . .
LISA: I know.
RITA: Well.
LISA: Are you all right?
RITA: Of course.
LISA: Good . . . I should go.
RITA: Yes.
LISA: The kids.
RITA: Of course. —Wait. Call me later. Will you? I don't think
   you should be alone.
LISA: I will.

(Lisa gathers her things, kisses Rita on the cheek, then exits. Rita sits in the chair. She picks up her decorating magazine and looks at a page—but then, she realizes she has something to say.)

RITA: Ben. Our children are a disaster. Lonely and terrible . . . I
   blame you . . . Of course, I was there. So I can't, in all fair-
   ness, lay all the debris at your feet. I was there. I watched.
   I watched it all, and I remember everything. I do. I remember the first time I saw you. I was with a friend, we were
   so young, and you walked over to the car and the sun was
   behind you so I couldn't see your face. But as soon as I did.
   I could see, right then, that first moment, that you loved me
   . . . And I was trapped. And I tried, for a very long time and
   with all my might, to love you back. I remember the very

first time you ever touched me . . . I remember sitting, by myself, in the dark, in the middle of the night. I remember your face, so dark and hard, like metal. And although I've tried, I *don't* remember, when it happened, the moment when I started hating you. I've searched and searched. I've looked in every corner, but I can't find it. I suppose it isn't really there. No moment. No single second when it happened. It was slow and inevitable, like getting old. I didn't hear it happen, and then I noticed that it had. It had to. And all you ever did was love someone you thought I was . . . And now you get to leave . . . And I am . . . so frightened. You've been my work for all these years. And I have never been alone.

(She starts to cry.)

I don't know what to do, or what I am.

(She sits there for a moment, still, crying, looking at her husband. Curtis appears in the doorway. He looks at his parents for a moment. And then . . .)

CURTIS: Is he dead?

(She smiles, so pleased at the sound of his voice. She looks at him.)

RITA: Maybe tomorrow.

(Blackout.)

Act Two

Scene 1
LOCATION, LOCATION, LOCATION

An empty apartment. One large room, with a kitchen along the wall and a door to a bathroom. There is some debris on the floor, in a corner: some magazines, a few paper coffee cups. Brian enters, dressed for business. He's followed by Curtis, who is dressed more casually. Brian turns on the lights.

BRIAN: Well. As you can see, it's move-in ready.

CURTIS: Except for the garbage.

BRIAN: Workmen.

CURTIS: Is that a northern exposure?

BRIAN: West.

CURTIS: So there's no morning sun.

BRIAN: No, but it gets the afternoon. You can't have everything. The view isn't half bad really. Trust me. If you shut your eyes you can see the Chrysler building.

CURTIS: Pardon me?

BRIAN: I was making a joke. A little real-estate humor. There isn't much of a view. But the price is right.

CURTIS: Maybe.

BRIAN: I think the bed would work along this wall, and you could screen off the kitchen area.

CURTIS: I could.

BRIAN: I'm told the seller's *very* motivated.

(Curtis looks around.)

CURTIS: Is it noisy? What do you think? I mean the traffic. I work at home so that's important.

BRIAN: I can't imagine noise'll be a problem. You're five flights up—and you're right next door to the Unitarian church.

CURTIS: Are they quiet?

BRIAN: I'm told they are. And as I said, the seller's ready to deal.

CURTIS: Why?

BRIAN: The market. You must know what's happening out there. It's a bloodbath. A year ago you could sell a lean-to on the FDR for a million-five. Now everyone expects a bargain. Don't you watch the news?

CURTIS: It depresses me.

BRIAN: Well, it can be grim.

CURTIS: Not the news, per se, although you're right that can be grim, but the people who read it—they depress me. "The newscasters."

BRIAN: Oh?

CURTIS: They're all so pretty, you know? It's like they have perfect teeth, and perfect hair—and perfect *lives*. Like giant Ken dolls spitting out tragedy.

BRIAN: What do you do again?

CURTIS: I write.

BRIAN: Not the news, I take it.

CURTIS: No, no. Short stories.

BRIAN: . . . You know they're asking six-fifty?

CURTIS: I have other income.

BRIAN: I didn't mean to imply—

CURTIS: It's fine. You're exactly right. Writing short stories in this day and age is like making Victrolas. People might think they're beautiful, or fascinating, and they look good in a room—but no one has any real interest. It's a losing proposition.

BRIAN: Still, it must be exciting.

CURTIS: Why is that?

BRIAN: I don't know. Being creative. It must be exciting to start with nothing, just a blank piece of paper and create a whole world.

CURTIS: You'd be surprised how *un*creative I can be. And there's no paper anymore.

BRIAN: Right.

CURTIS: It's computers now.

BRIAN: I know. —But, still metaphorically.

CURTIS: "Metaphorically"? You went to college, I see.

BRIAN: Is that a big word?

CURTIS: Everything is relative.

BRIAN: I went to SUNY, at Purchase.

CURTIS: Really? What was your major? I mean what does one study to prepare for the fast-paced and cut-throat world of glamorous Manhattan real estate?

BRIAN: Acting.

CURTIS: Of course.

BRIAN: Yes, I'm one of the ten million people in this city who call themselves an actor.

CURTIS: Could I have seen you in something?

BRIAN: I doubt it.

CURTIS: Try me. You might be surprised. I'm an avid follower of the arts. Have you been in something?

BRIAN: Just an evening of one-acts at EST.

CURTIS: I've been there!

BRIAN: Really?

CURTIS: Lots of stairs and the smell of urine?

BRIAN: That's right! But respected. I mean people respect it. I was in last year's marathon series, Night B. The third play.

CURTIS: I only saw Night A.

BRIAN: Oh. Well, it was a crappy part.

CURTIS: I'm sure you were great.

BRIAN: I don't know about that. I mean my senior year at Purchase I was doing Happy in *Salesman*, and five years later I'm a waiter in a one-act. Not exactly a staggering trajectory.

CURTIS: Maybe you're not very talented.

BRIAN (*Light-hearted*): Fuck you.

CURTIS: I didn't say you weren't. I've never seen you. For all I know you're Olivier with biceps.

BRIAN: It's not easy, you know? A lot of it's luck. And the right agent.

CURTIS: Of course.

BRIAN: I had an agent who really believed in me. She was fantastic—

CURTIS: What happened?

BRIAN: Alcohol poisoning.

CURTIS: I see.

BRIAN: And since then . . . well.

CURTIS: Thus the real estate.

BRIAN: Exactly. Thus.

CURTIS: It must be frustrating.

BRIAN: Something'll turn up. It's important to run your own race. And I go on meetings, auditions. I send out my photo.

CURTIS: The one on the website?

BRIAN: What website?

CURTIS: The real-estate website. The agency.

BRIAN: Oh, yeah—right. That's my headshot. Commercial. I have something much more serious for theater.

CURTIS: It doesn't really look like you.

BRIAN: I didn't think so either!

CURTIS: You're a lot better looking in person. I hope that's okay—

(Beat.)

BRIAN: Did I tell you the maintenance?

CURTIS: Maintenance?

BRIAN: On the apartment.

CURTIS: Oh. Eight-something.

BRIAN: Eight-twenty-five.

CURTIS: That seems a little high.

BRIAN: It's average. Really. For the neighborhood. Did you notice the height of the ceilings? And we're only a block from the subway. I expect this one to go pretty fast, even in the current market.

CURTIS: You know, I'm at CAA—

BRIAN: What?

CURTIS: As a writer. They represent me.

BRIAN: Really?

CURTIS: Maybe I could talk to someone.

BRIAN: About what?

CURTIS: About you.

BRIAN: What do you mean?

CURTIS: Well, I can't promise anything. But I could talk to someone, make an inquiry—

BRIAN *(Excited)*: You mean an agent? Talk to an agent? About
me?

CURTIS: I'm not making a promise.

BRIAN: *That would be amazing!*

CURTIS: I don't actually know anyone on that end.

BRIAN: But you think you could—

CURTIS: My agent must know them.

BRIAN: I would die!

CURTIS: Don't do that.

BRIAN: I mean it! I would die!

CURTIS: I could talk to him, my agent. See what he can do.

BRIAN: That would be fantastic!

CURTIS: Well, we'll see. I said, I can't make any promises. We
haven't been getting along lately. My agent and me.

BRIAN: Oh?

CURTIS: We had a disagreement and he said some terrible
things. But listen, I'll do it. I'll swallow my pride and give
him a call.

BRIAN: That would be great!

CURTIS: I'll do it Monday.

BRIAN: God. Really, thank you.

(Beat.)

CURTIS: Has this been on the market long?

BRIAN: Why would you do that?

CURTIS: Do what?

BRIAN: Call your agent—I mean, about me. Why would you do
that? I'm just curious.

CURTIS: Why wouldn't I?

BRIAN: You don't even know me. You don't know if I'm any good. I could be completely without talent. I'm not by the way. But I could be.

CURTIS: No one is *completely* without talent.

BRIAN: You know what I mean.

CURTIS: I have a sixth sense. I knew the minute I looked at you—

BRIAN: I don't understand why you would do it—extend yourself for me, really. I'm a stranger. We just met.

CURTIS: Can't I be generous?

BRIAN: You think I can get them to drop the price, don't you? That's it, isn't it?

CURTIS: I can't believe . . .

BRIAN: You think I can get you a better price. Is that why? I already told you the seller was motivated. I can only do so much. They're asking six-fifty—I think they'll take six. But I can't do more than that. So I mean, if you think that dangling an agent in front of me is going to get you some kind of fantastic—

CURTIS: You're very cynical.

BRIAN: I'm just asking.

CURTIS: You're accusing.

BRIAN: You think I'll waive my commission, then. Is that the angle?

CURTIS: No.

BRIAN: Admit it.

CURTIS: I was just being friendly!

BRIAN: I can't waive my commission. First of all I need it to live and secondly I work for an agency. They won't just let me waive a commission.

CURTIS: Why do you assume I have an *angle*?

BRIAN: Because I'm not stupid.

CURTIS: No, I know that. You went to Purchase.

BRIAN: Is it sex? Am I supposed to suck your dick or something?

CURTIS: Oh my god!

BRIAN: You have to admit it's odd, I mean it's unexpected that a total stranger would just—

CURTIS: I made an offer, a friendly offer! What does it cost me to make a phone call? Nothing! I make a gesture of kindness toward you and you turn around and ascribe to it the most vile motives, disgusting motives.

BRIAN: Okay—

CURTIS: I don't want anything! I didn't *expect* anything. I was being generous!

BRIAN: I'm sorry—

CURTIS: It may be hard to believe, and maybe you don't recognize it in today's world, but I was being friendly! That's all! That's it! . . . Christ.

BRIAN: I'm sorry.

CURTIS: You have a dyspeptic view of mankind.

BRIAN *(Apologetic)*: I guess.

CURTIS: God.

BRIAN: I'm sorry. Really.

CURTIS: All right fine. Let's—let's just forget it.

(Beat.)

BRIAN: I'm an idiot. A fucking idiot. Fuck me. Fuck me!

CURTIS: It's over now.

BRIAN: You do something nice and I—I am terrible at reading people. That's probably why I'm so bad at this, this real-estate thing. I have like the lowest sales numbers at the branch. You know, I started at the same time as this girl, we trained together. She has a lazy eye and she's not very pretty, and believe it or not, she has zoomed past me. I tell myself it's luck, but it's not. She's good. She can read people. She can size them up. She would never've insulted you the way I did.

CURTIS: You didn't insult me.

BRIAN: I basically accused you of blackmail.

CURTIS: I overreacted.

BRIAN: You had every right.

CURTIS: Let's just forget it, all right. It never happened. We'll start from scratch.

BRIAN: Really?

CURTIS: Please.

BRIAN: So . . . we're cool?

CURTIS: While, I'm not a person who uses the word "cool," except to mean the chilly side of temperate—I would say yes. We're cool.

BRIAN: Good. *(Beat, then sheepish)* So, you'll make the call?

CURTIS *(Very amused)*: Well, now I feel swindled.

BRIAN: Okay, okay, forget it.

CURTIS: No, it's fine.

BRIAN: Don't call him. I don't want you to.

CURTIS: I'm going to call him.

BRIAN: You will?

CURTIS: Yes.

BRIAN: Don't.

CURTIS: I'm going to.

BRIAN: Really?

CURTIS: Yes.

BRIAN: Thank you. And again, I apologize.

(A moment passes.)

CURTIS *(Looking around)*: So, what do they want down?

BRIAN: Y'know, actually, I could talk to my boss. If things work out maybe I could cut the commission by like five points or something.

CURTIS: Suit yourself. —Is the floor oak or—or what is it?

BRIAN *(Offering)*: You want a piece of gum?

CURTIS: No thank you.

BRIAN: Do you mind if I . . . ?

CURTIS: Of course not.

BRIAN *(Putting a piece of gum in his mouth)*: We're not supposed to chew gum, when we show apartments. They say it's unprofessional. They're very strict, they're bullies. They tell us what to wear, what to say—and sometimes they send out spies. People who pretend to look at apartments, but really they're just supposed to trap us in some kind of "unprofessional behavior."

CURTIS: Really?

BRIAN: A guy got fired last week 'cause he used the word motherfucker when he was showing an apartment.

CURTIS: In what context?

BRIAN: He slammed a door on his hand.

CURTIS: Oh. Well, it seems called for.

BRIAN: So, why're you moving anyway?

CURTIS: I've been renting and it's time to buy. I have to say I like this place. For me.

BRIAN: It's okay.

CURTIS: It's right for now, but what happens if I meet someone? I mean, it's okay for me, but I can't imagine two people—

BRIAN: You could trade up.

CURTIS: With two people you need rooms. Actual rooms.

BRIAN: Tell me about it. I live with my girlfriend—*we're* in a studio, and it is not easy. Let me tell you —

CURTIS: Oh?

BRIAN (*Shrugging*): But it's what we can afford.

(Curtis moves away from him. Beat.)

You know what, if you buy this place or even if you don't, I think this is it. I think this is my farewell to real estate.

CURTIS: Really?

BRIAN: I can't do it. I can't keep doing this.

CURTIS: You're not happy?

BRIAN: Who could be happy? I mean it's basically immoral. Like my offer to trim the commission. I don't have to talk to my boss. We're *supposed* to cut our commissions. The market's as dry as the Amazon.

CURTIS: You mean the Mojave?

BRIAN: And I happen to know that there's a leak. In that corner. They didn't fix it. They just painted over the water stains!

CURTIS: It's looking less and less like a bargain.

BRIAN: It's not a big leak. You could fix it. But they didn't. That's the point. My girlfriend thought I'd be good at this. She said, "You're an actor, sell real estate. It should be easy." What it is, is a nightmare. And I'm not good at it and that's the fact. —Success breeds success and I got shit.

CURTIS: What's her name?

BRIAN: Who?

CURTIS: Your girlfriend. It's just— You've mentioned her twice now, in as many minutes.

BRIAN: Dawn.

CURTIS: Oh, that's a beautiful name.

BRIAN: Yeah.

CURTIS: What does she do?

BRIAN: She's an actress.

CURTIS: Is it serious?

BRIAN *(Hedging)*: Well, I don't—

CURTIS: I'm just curious.

BRIAN: I think so. I think it is. Maybe it is.

CURTIS: Do you love her?

BRIAN: What?

CURTIS: Do you love her?

BRIAN: Well, I mean, that's sort of personal, don't you—

CURTIS: I'm sorry. I am. I'm a writer. I guess I'm just naturally
   curious. I try to find out about people.

BRIAN: Right.

CURTIS: Do you? Love her?

   (Beat.)

BRIAN: I do. I think. I think I love her.

CURTIS: Describe her.

BRIAN: What?

CURTIS: What does she look like?

BRIAN: Um. Brown hair. Blue eyes.

CURTIS: Is she tall?

BRIAN: No.

CURTIS: Short.

BRIAN: Average.

CURTIS: Where did you meet?

BRIAN: Acting class.

CURTIS: Is she talented?

BRIAN *(Considering this)*: Yeah. Yes, she is. She's talented.

CURTIS: Did you love her right away?

BRIAN: I don't remember.

CURTIS: Is she funny.

BRIAN: Sometimes.

CURTIS: Is she good in bed?

BRIAN: What?

CURTIS: Is she good in bed?

BRIAN: Wait a minute—

CURTIS *(Becoming aggressive)*: Is she good in bed?

BRIAN: Where is this going? I mean, we're standing around—

CURTIS *(Very firm)*: Just answer. Answer the question. Is she?

BRIAN *(Defensive)*: She's fine.

CURTIS: Fine?

BRIAN: She's great.

CURTIS: Does she love you?

BRIAN: I don't know.

CURTIS: But you fuck her.

BRIAN: Okay, stop it.

CURTIS: You fuck her a lot.

BRIAN: Shut up!

CURTIS: How do you fuck her?

BRIAN: What is with you, man!? What the fuck is wrong with you?!

CURTIS: Are you on top?!

BRIAN: You don't just ask that!

CURTIS: Is she on top? How do you fuck her? Describe it to me!

BRIAN: Shut the fuck up!!

CURTIS *(Vicious)*: Do you fuck her in the ass!?

BRIAN: Stop it!!

CURTIS: She lets you fuck her in the ass?!

BRIAN: What the fuck is wrong with you?!

CURTIS: Answer the question.

BRIAN: Fuck you!

CURTIS: You want me to buy this apartment?

BRIAN: I don't care!

CURTIS: I'll buy this apartment.

BRIAN: I don't give a shit!!

CURTIS: Of course you do! You and your girlfriend, you and Dawn, of the medium height, of the brown hair and the blue eyes, the two of you, you and Dawn, who lets you fuck her in the ass, or doesn't let you fuck her in the ass—the two of you jammed into that tiny room with no walls, one room! I think you need this sale! I think you really need it! I think you'd say anything! Any goddamn thing that enters your fucking little mind!

BRIAN: *What the fuck is wrong with you!!?*

(Curtis's cell phone rings. They look at each other, tense. A moment passes. It rings again. Brian walks away as Curtis answers it.)

CURTIS: Hello . . . Hi . . . Oh . . . No, I don't think so . . . Yes.

(A moment passes before Curtis closes his phone. And another before he puts it back in his pocket.

He tries to repress it, but the call has clearly affected Curtis very, very deeply.)

My father died.

BRIAN: What?

CURTIS: Just now. That was my mother. She called to tell me.

BRIAN: Holy shit.

CURTIS: It doesn't matter. I mean it's not a shock. It was expected.

BRIAN: Oh.

CURTIS: In fact, it was expected a week ago. I said good-bye a week ago. I sat there for two days, in that room, with my mother. And he wouldn't die.

BRIAN: Oh.

CURTIS: Now I missed it.

BRIAN *(Quiet)*: . . . Listen. I'm going to leave you my card—

CURTIS: What?

(Brian puts his business card on the floor.)

BRIAN: I'm gonna go. But take as long as you want. Look around. Whatever. Just shut the door when you're finished. Okay?

(Curtis nods.)

Are you okay?

CURTIS: I'm fine.

BRIAN: Take as long as you want.

CURTIS: I'm trying to figure out why you would lie.

BRIAN: You mean, what, about the leak?

CURTIS: No. No, I don't mean about the leak. I mean about everything.

BRIAN: I don't understand.

CURTIS: I don't think there is anyone named Dawn.

BRIAN: She's my girlfriend.

CURTIS: I think I know why.

BRIAN: We live together.

CURTIS *(Broken)*: I think you lied, I think you invented her to *avoid* me. I mean, you wanted the sale. You want me to call my agent, to get you an agent. And I think, you thought, if I thought you were gay, you might be expected to do things. With me. So you found a way to make all of that moot. I don't blame you. Not really. Although it was stupid. It was pointless. Because nothing would have happened.

BRIAN: Dawn is my girlfriend. We live together.

CURTIS: *I don't think that's true!*

BRIAN: I'm gonna go.

CURTIS : I think your name is Brian Hutchins. And you live at 163 West 83rd Street. You live on the sixth floor, in the front apartment. And you date men.

BRIAN *(Stunned)*: . . . Who are you?

CURTIS: I think you had sex, last night, with a man. Dark hair. Maybe Spanish. He was wearing a red sweatshirt.

BRIAN *(Quiet)*: Holy fucking god.

CURTIS: He was there from eight-thirty, until ten-thirty. You had sex, and then he left. He got in a taxi. And you watched the news. Until you went to bed.

BRIAN: Who are you?

CURTIS *(Fragile)*: I'm just someone, who happens to live at 164, West 83rd Street. On the sixth floor . . . In the front apartment.

BRIAN *(Horrified)*: Oh my god.

CURTIS: Do you think, in a million years, that I would buy this apartment, this shitty apartment, with its leaks and its northern exposure!?

BRIAN: You watched me?

CURTIS: I have been. Watching. For a long time.

BRIAN: Fucking Christ.

CURTIS: Until this week, your name was Peter. In my head. I named you Peter . . . And I loved you very much. And we never fought.

BRIAN: Sick motherfucking . . .

CURTIS: Only yesterday I looked at your name on the buzzer and I searched until I found your face, on a real-estate website.

(Brian approaches Curtis.)

BRIAN *(A threat)*: Stay the fuck away from me.

CURTIS: Answer my question.

BRIAN *(Cruel)*: I don't answer your fucking questions!

CURTIS: Am I right?

BRIAN: Fucking pervert!

CURTIS: Is that why you lied?

BRIAN: You better move!

CURTIS: Was I right?!

BRIAN: Find another place to live!

CURTIS: Is that why?!!

BRIAN: You understand me?! Find another place!

CURTIS *(Standing his ground)*: NO.

BRIAN: I WILL FUCKING KILL YOU!

CURTIS: I'M NOT GOING ANYWHERE.

BRIAN: I MEAN IT.

CURTIS *(A challenge)*: FUCK YOU!

> *(Brian hits him hard, in the stomach. Curtis doubles over in pain. Brian hits him again in the stomach, and then on the back of the head. Curtis falls to the ground. Brian kicks him, twice, hard. And then looks at him.)*

BRIAN: Shut the door on your way out.

> *(Brian exits. Blackout.)*

Scene 2
MOST POOR SONS OF BITCHES

The lights come up on another hospital room, or the same hospital room. Curtis is in the bed, looking somewhat bored and annoyed. After a moment, the Nurse enters, carrying a food tray, which she puts in front of him. Her patience is short.

NURSE: Here you are.

CURTIS: What time is it?

NURSE: Four-thirty.

CURTIS: Four-thirty. I see. So what meal is this?

NURSE *(Obviously)*: Dinner.

CURTIS: Who *on god's green earth* eats dinner at four-thirty?

NURSE *(Strict)*: People in hospitals.

CURTIS: Well, it's insane.

NURSE: You're not gonna eat?

CURTIS: If I don't eat it, I won't get anything until tomorrow. I'll starve to death. I'll die.

NURSE: I don't think so. You're in a hospital. We wouldn't let that happen.

CURTIS: I was speaking hyperbolically.

(Beat. She runs a thermometer across his forehead, then reads it. He has no fever. She notes that on his chart.)

NURSE: Does your incision hurt?

CURTIS: No, it feels fantastic. My single regret is that I only have one spleen you people can rip out of me.

NURSE: Please, you were lucky. All that internal bleeding and it turned out to be something so useless.

CURTIS: Lucky me.

NURSE *(Bossy)*: I've seen people come in here looking better than you and go out in plastic bags.

CURTIS: Well, that's comforting.

NURSE: It happens all the time. Mr. Cornfield, down the hall, came in here with shortness of breath, three days later they were fitting him for a box.

CURTIS: Wonderful.

NURSE: This is a hospital. There's death around every corner. So you're missing a spleen? So what? The earth continues to spin.

CURTIS: Are you the only nurse on this floor?

NURSE: Just eat.

CURTIS: Couldn't they assign me someone a little less . . . jaundiced? I'm not asking for someone cheerful, I'll settle for quiet.

NURSE: You just want to complain.

CURTIS: I thought you were nice when you took care of my father. You seemed like the picture of silent efficiency.

NURSE: Are you gonna eat?

CURTIS: What would it take to put you *back* in your shell?

NURSE: Personally, it makes no difference to me, but it's my job to see that you do.

CURTIS *(Sighing)*: What is it?

NURSE: Salisbury steak.

CURTIS: I've had the Salisbury steak.

NURSE: What does that mean?

CURTIS: The cuisine here makes me wonder why they stopped me from bleeding to death in the first place.

NURSE: You think you're amusing?

CURTIS: I have moments.

NURSE: You're exhausting.

CURTIS: Says you.

NURSE *(Snappish)*: You *have* to eat.

CURTIS: No, I don't. Not that. It's disgusting.

NURSE: You'll want it later, when it's cold and congealed.

CURTIS: Never.

NURSE: And then you'll be sorry.

CURTIS: Well, we'll just see.

NURSE: I should take it away. That would teach you. There's nothing to eat in here. It's not like you've been showered with gift baskets, now is it? It's not like your relatives have sent fruit towers. I've seen homeless people with more generous friends.

CURTIS: I'd like a club sandwich.

NURSE: What?

CURTIS: I want a club sandwich. Turkey, white toast, mayonnaise.

NURSE: Where do you think you are?

CURTIS: And not that turkey roll. Not that pressed crap. I want turkey breast. Real turkey.

NURSE: You're in a hospital, not a delicatessen.

CURTIS: I'm not eating! I'm not eating until I get what I want!

NURSE: Yes, you will.

CURTIS: I won't! It's official, *I* am on a hunger strike! Do you hear me? Stand by with a glucose drip, because I'm not going to touch that. I mean it. I will not eat. I will not!

NURSE: You get hungry, you'll eat.

CURTIS: We'll just see won't we!?

NURSE: There's nothing wrong with your dinner. It's perfectly fine.

CURTIS: Don't you have other people to torture?

NURSE: Mr. Lyons, I have tried very hard to maintain a professional demeanor. But you are testing me. And I will not be tested. Do you understand? Do you understand me? You are going to eat that dinner!

CURTIS: Who do you think you're talking to? Who the fuck do you think you're talking to?!

(They glower at each other for a moment.)

NURSE *(A threat)*: When I come back, I expect that to be gone.

(She exits.)

CURTIS *(Calling after her)*: You call this bedside manner!?

(Ben enters from the wings, dressed casually, and addresses the audience. Curtis neither sees nor hears him.)

BEN: Dying, as you'd expect, turned out to be not all that exciting. I was asleep when it happened. One minute I was
dreaming of rabbits and then all at once, nothing. I don't
mind it here, wherever I am. We don't call it heaven—
but we don't call it hell. It's all right—although the lines
for *everything* are incredibly long. I was scared, of course,
at first. But then this man came up to me, this old man.
I didn't know him. He was old. And very small. And his skin
was gray. I didn't speak. And then he put his arms around
me. And I smelled him. And I knew. He found me . . . My
father found me. And I wasn't afraid.

(Rita appears in the doorway.)

RITA *(To Curtis)*: Are you up?
CURTIS: I'm awake.
RITA: How are you feeling?
BEN *(To Rita)*: People smell like who they are!

*(Ben exits as Rita breezes into the room. She is wearing a black
dress and holding a floral arrangement, which she places on the
windowsill.)*

RITA: You look better, so much better. You look fine. You're losing that eggy pallor you had yesterday. Your sister's right
behind me. She stopped to say hello to that nice young man
down the hall.
CURTIS: What nice young man?
RITA: Leonard something. I told you about him.
CURTIS: The one who's dying?
RITA: Lymphoma. She went to his room by accident, the day
they brought you in. She thought it was your room. And
they struck up conversation. I think there's a spark—she
could do worse. She's done worse.

CURTIS: He's *dying*!

RITA: People aren't perfect, Curtis. You expect too much. I think that's why your boyfriends have all been imaginary. You create them so you can make them perfect.

CURTIS: As it happens, they weren't perfect.

RITA: Really?

CURTIS: Ethan, for instance, had a lateral lisp.

RITA: How could you tell?

CURTIS: I don't want to talk about it.

RITA: Hmmm.

CURTIS: How was the funeral?

RITA: The police called again this morning.

CURTIS: What did you tell them?

RITA: I told them it was up to you.

CURTIS: Good.

RITA: That you must have your reasons. They think I can get you to cooperate. I assured them I can get you to do nothing.

CURTIS: I want to let it go. All right? I want to put it behind me.

RITA: I still don't understand what you were doing in that empty apartment to begin with.

CURTIS: I told you! A drug buy.

RITA: A drug buy? Really? A drug buy? What kind of lingo is that? You don't do drugs and since when do you talk like a character from *Cagney & Lacey*?

CURTIS: I wanted to experiment.

RITA: You're too old to start experimenting. Stick with things you know. Is that your dinner? I'm starving.

(Rita lifts the lid on Curtis's dinner, takes the Jell-O, restores the lid and eats the Jell-O.)

CURTIS: What did they say?

RITA: Who?

CURTIS *(Slightly annoyed)*: The police.

RITA: They want you to press charges. They want you to look at pictures.

CURTIS: Absolutely not. I want to pretend the whole thing never happened.

(Lisa appears in the doorway, wearing a black dress.)

LISA: Hello?

RITA: Come in, dear.

LISA *(To Curtis)*: How are you feeling?

CURTIS: The same.

LISA: We shouldn't stay too long. The sitter's on the clock and Raymond is waiting.

RITA: He should come up.

LISA: I told him.

CURTIS: Who the hell is Raymond?

RITA: Her sponsor. Since she fell off the wagon last week he's been on her like flies on paper. They've both been staying at the house. It's been fun really—except for all that "testifying."

LISA: He's new. He's my new sponsor.

CURTIS: What happened to your old one?

LISA: He stopped returning my calls. But Raymond is very sweet and better looking. He understands that this is a very tricky time. I need *constant* supervision.

RITA: How's Leonard, dear?

LISA: They just put in a Hickman catheter.

RITA: Isn't that nice? That's nice. You're a sweet couple.

CURTIS: It doesn't bother *anyone* that this guy's about to expire!?

LISA: It would, I suppose, under normal circumstances. But these aren't normal circumstances. I'm feeling very vulnerable.

CURTIS: Still!

LISA: Did I tell you David called? He did. He asked if he could bring someone to the funeral. Bring someone! Can you believe that? I told him I was driving through a tunnel and then I hung up. —He brought a date to his ex-father-in-law's funeral!

RITA: Very bad taste. Is there more Jell-O?

(Rita checks. There is none. She restores the lid.)

LISA: She was dressed like a floozy. I hate him. I do, I mean it. *(To Rita)* Did they look happy? I don't think they looked happy. Maybe it won't last.

RITA: He beat the crap out of you, dear. Let it go.

CURTIS: How *was* the funeral?

RITA: I thought more people would show up. But it looks like rain. I suppose the weather kept them away.

CURTIS: And the fact that no one very much liked the deceased.

RITA: It was touching, really. And, I feel, somehow important. You know I never said good-bye—when it happened. I missed it. Did I tell you that? I was sleeping. I sat there day after day, waiting, watching him. Asleep. Awake. Hour after hour. And then I drifted off. And then it happened. And so I missed it.

LISA: Who brings a date to a funeral?

RITA: Your Uncle Seth was there. He's fat now.

CURTIS: He was always fat.

RITA: Well, he's fat-er. He looks like a white Mills Brother.

LISA: Who?

RITA: But it was a charming service. I cried beautifully and Lisa read a poem by e. e. cummings.

CURTIS *(To Lisa)*: Why on earth?

LISA: I have no idea.

CURTIS *(Ironic)*: It sounds very nice.

RITA: I'm having your father cremated. I have a catalog in my purse and I thought we could vote on an urn. I'm thinking something very ginger jar.

CURTIS: Maybe later.

LISA: I'll look!

(Rita hands Lisa a catalog from her purse. Lisa leafs through it. The Nurse enters.)

NURSE: Did you eat?

CURTIS: No.

NURSE: I'll be back.

(The Nurse exits.)

CURTIS *(A confidence)*: She hates me.

RITA: What are you talking about?

CURTIS: She seems pleasant enough—but the reality is, behind closed doors, she's a Nazi.

RITA: Well. Have you been friendly to her?

CURTIS: Of course.

RITA: You have?

CURTIS: Why wouldn't I be friendly?

RITA: Have you shown an interest?

CURTIS: Yes.

RITA: Really?

CURTIS: Yes!

RITA: What's her name?

CURTIS *(No idea)*: . . . I've been *very* friendly!

RITA: You don't even know her name.

CURTIS: Of course I do! It's Eunice!

RITA: You're making that up.

CURTIS: Of course I am.

RITA: You see?

LISA *(Regarding an urn in the catalog)*: I like this one.

RITA *(Looking)*: Vile.

LISA: It's sweet.

RITA: It has antelopes all over it.

LISA: I like them.

RITA: No. Absolutely not. No, antelopes.

LISA *(Pouting)*: Fine.

(Lisa resumes browsing the catalog.)

CURTIS *(To Lisa)*: Why do you take her side? I mean, I tell you the woman is nasty and you blame me.

RITA *(Ignoring that)*: Curtis, have you thought about what we discussed?

CURTIS: What we discussed?

RITA: Your coming to live with me.

CURTIS: Oh Christ.

RITA: You're going to need someone. You're going to be recuperating. You can't look after yourself.

CURTIS: I have so far.

RITA: And where did it get you? Bleeding on the floor of a vacant apartment, that's where. You're not exactly a tower of self-sufficiency, are you? I don't mean you should live with me forever. Just for a while. A few weeks. A few years—

CURTIS *(To himself)*: Oh my god.

RITA: Until you're on your feet again. In the past you've always said you couldn't. You had Peter to think of. But now that he's evaporated I don't see how you can turn down my—

CURTIS: NO! . . . No. I will not live with you. I cannot make my feelings on this subject any clearer. It was bad enough that I was sentenced to live with you for the first eighteen years of my life. But I've been paroled and, trust me, I'm not going back!

RITA: I remember only good times.

CURTIS: Then you've had a lobotomy. I refuse to relive the Hindenburg of my childhood. Just accept the fact I am not going to live with you. Not for a month. Not for a day. Not for an hour! I realize you're afraid to be alone. But maybe you should have thought of that before you came at me with a letter opener when I was seven. Or crept into my room, in tears, in the middle of the night. Or threatened to send me to foster parents if I didn't go *antiquing* with you! So, for the last time, I will not visit, cohabitate or rehabilitate in your home! *So please, once and for all, dear god, let the subject die a natural death!!*

RITA: Do you want to think about it?

CURTIS: NO!!

RITA: Fine.

(Beat. Rita gathers herself.)

In that case, I think you should read this.

(Rita produces a letter from her purse. He takes it.)

CURTIS: What is it?

RITA: A letter.

CURTIS: I see that. What's it got to do with me?

RITA: Lisa, pay attention.

LISA: What?

RITA: I've made a decision.

LISA: About the urn?

RITA: About my life.

CURTIS *(Regarding the letter)*: Who is this from?

RITA: Just read it.

(He opens the letter and looks at it.)

CURTIS: I can't. This handwriting is terrible.

RITA: It's from Raymond.

LISA: *My* Raymond?

RITA: I don't think of him as *your* Raymond.

LISA: My sponsor, my new sponsor—who's been staying with us?

RITA: The very same.

LISA: He's writing you letters? Why is he writing you letters?

CURTIS: What's going on?

RITA: Read it.

CURTIS: I said I can't.

RITA: Then I'll tell you what it says.

LISA: Why would he write to you?

RITA: I found this letter on my dressing table yesterday morning. In it Raymond tells me that he thinks I'm funny. He thinks I'm vivacious and witty and that I have an unparalleled zest for living.

LISA *(Snatching the letter)*: Give me that!

RITA: It's true. He says that getting to know me has been one of the great joys of his life.

LISA: My Raymond?!

CURTIS: You?

RITA: That's right. And that he cares for me.

CURTIS: He says all that?

RITA: More or less.

LISA: I can't make out a word.

CURTIS: How old is this guy?

LISA: He's forty-something!

RITA: Is it so unbelievable that he should care for me?

CURTIS: Is that rhetorical?

LISA: When did this happen?! Where was I while this was going on? I've been there every day.

RITA: You do sleep, don't you?

CURTIS: Most people wait until *after* the funeral to begin seeing someone, but I suppose . . .

LISA: I feel very betrayed! Very hurt and very betrayed.

RITA: We didn't plan this. It just happened. Things happen. People meet, there are sparks—

LISA: You're saying you've had sex with him? You've slept with Raymond!?

RITA: That's none of your business! Yes.

LISA: Oh my god!

RITA: He thought it might upset you.

LISA: He told me he couldn't get an erection because he had diabetes.

RITA: He told me that he told you that.

CURTIS: You're having sex with some forty year old? Who *are* you?!

RITA: I'm the same person I've always been. And I waited until your father was *almost* dead.

CURTIS: Do you have feelings for this Raymond?

RITA: Please don't call him "this Raymond."

CURTIS: Do you?

RITA *(Dismissive)*: He's fine. He's nice looking.

LISA: I feel sick.

CURTIS *(To Rita)*: But you believe he has feelings for you.

RITA: Of course not.

CURTIS: What?

RITA: I'm not stupid, Curtis. But neither is Raymond. He can spot an opportunity.

LISA: What does that mean?

RITA: Raymond is an artist. A painter, to be exact. He's a cross between David Hockney and Willem de Kooning.

CURTIS: It sounds awful.

RITA: It is. He says his art would improve if he didn't have to work for a living.

LISA: Raymond? My Raymond?

RITA: Yes, dear. The very first night he came to the house—you were asleep—he opened up to me over an Entenmann's coffee ring and we talked. We talked for hours. He ended up crying, about something. I don't know what. I wasn't really paying attention . . . And I took him to my bed.

LISA: *Oh my god!*

CURTIS: You're a middle-aged matron! What are you doing taking strange men, men you don't even know, to your bed? It's, it's—unseemly. It's disgusting!

RITA: I'm ignoring that.

LISA: But—

RITA: The point is, we're going to Aruba.

LISA: Aruba!?

CURTIS: When?!

RITA: Tonight.

CURTIS: You're serious!?

RITA: Yes. If you'd said you wanted to recuperate with me, I would have postponed. But you didn't.

LISA: I can't believe this!

RITA: It's true. We discussed it this morning, while you were in the shower. There's a flight tonight, out of JFK, and we're going to be on it.

CURTIS: Don't you think it's in sort of bad taste?! I mean, the very day of your husband's funeral you run off with a man you've known for a week?!

RITA: I really don't care.

LISA: I need a sponsor!

RITA: He'll make a call.

CURTIS: How long will you be gone?

RITA: Indefinitely.

LISA: What does that mean!?

RITA: It means a long time. I don't know how long. But a long time.

LISA: You're just running away?!

RITA: More or less.

LISA: I can't breathe.

RITA: I'm starting over. I'm beginning again. I'm not so old that I should just give up.

CURTIS: You know he only wants your money. He may say "zest for life" but he means big fat bank account.

RITA: Of course I know that. And that brings me to the second part of my announcement. Curtis, you're going to have to find another way to live.

CURTIS: What do you mean?

RITA: It was fine for me to give you money when your father was alive—

LISA: You gave him money?!

RITA: But your father left less than I expected, and if I'm going to keep Raymond happy I'll need every cent.

CURTIS: You're just cutting me off?

RITA: It's overdue, really.

CURTIS: Without warning?!

RITA: Let's be honest. Even if your short stories were wonderful, which they're not, there's no living to be made there. You've had a dozen years to write your way out of mediocre obscurity and you've failed. At a certain point it's time to face facts, consider your options and devise a new plan. I might feel differently if I thought you were talented, but I don't.

LISA: How much money did you give him?!

CURTIS: You don't think I'm talented!?

RITA: I know it's a shock—

CURTIS: It certainly is!

LISA: You can't do this!

CURTIS: You're just cutting me off?!

LISA: This is a very bad time—

CURTIS: Why? Why now?!

LISA: You cannot do this! I forbid you to!

RITA: I hoped you'd be happy for me.

LISA: I think it's selfish—incredibly selfish! We're your children. Our father's just died and you decide to take this moment and—

CURTIS: Have you thought this through?!

LISA *(Mumbled, to herself)*:

God grant me the serenity:
To accept the things I cannot change;
Courage to change the things I can;

And wisdom to know the difference.

CURTIS:

Why are you doing this? Can you tell me? Can you explain it to me? Tell me! Why are you doing this!!?

RITA *(Triumphant)*: BECAUSE I CAN! Because I have to! I think I have to! There is nothing for me here. Yes, to the naked eye, there are connections. I have children. I have friends. But my friends are strangers and my children are sad and unforgiving. Lisa, I cannot live, every day, under the mountain of tragedy you create. Your life is too treacherous and too exhausting. A cloud passes in front of the sun and you see Armageddon! Curtis, whatever your childhood was, it's an old book and the pages are faded. You refuse to forgive anyone for anything and it's enough! I realize you are who you are and I bear responsibility. But the days turn into years and it has to end! I'm doing this because I spent forty years in a marriage to a man I never loved. But even contempt is a connection—and now that's gone, and I am rootless in the world. I'm doing this because I'm still alive and I have to find a way to try to feel *something*! It may seem fast, or look abrupt, but that's the way the world is. You wait and wait and wait and then everything changes, all at once! And yes, I'm scared. I am scared to death. But I'm going to take this leap. Do you understand me?! I want to spend my time on the sand, in the sun, by the water, with a man too young for me, because I'm in a position to do it! Do I love him? No. Does he love me? I doubt it very much. But he's nice. And he thinks I'm funny and we aren't locked in some war that never ends! I'm sorry if you feel abandoned, but you're adults now and it's time. It's past time! Your father is gone and I *have* to become something else! Raymond is waiting for me. We are going to Aruba. Tonight! I'm going to fly away from this place and you and my life! I'm going to start over, all over! I am leaving! And you can shout bon voyage, or, frankly, you *can both go fuck yourselves.*

(Rita gets her purse.)

Lisa, you can pick any urn you want. Wish me luck.

(Rita exits. There is a long pause.)

CURTIS: Wow . . . He was right.

LISA: What?

CURTIS: She *is* a bitch.

LISA: . . . I can't believe it.

CURTIS: She doesn't think I'm talented.

LISA: How much money did she give you?

CURTIS: Let it go.

(Beat. They are both fairly devastated.)

LISA *(Fragile)*: She's gone.

CURTIS: Did you ever think . . . ?

LISA: Never.

CURTIS *(Forced)*: Well . . . Well. Good for her.

LISA: Hmmm.

(There's a pause. We can see that their mother's departure has made them both feel quite sad and a little empty. And then, Lisa has a great insight. She stands.)

I'm gonna go.

CURTIS: What?

LISA: I should go.

CURTIS: Wait. Stay for a while. You can call a cab.

LISA: No, really, I—

CURTIS: Just a little while.

LISA: I shouldn't.

CURTIS: Please?

LISA *(After a quick internal debate)*: I don't want to.

CURTIS: Oh.

LISA: I'm sorry.

CURTIS: Why should you? I mean, really, why should you? It's not like we're friends. We've never been friends. Really.

LISA: I'm sorry about that.

CURTIS: You want to go home.

LISA *(Becoming happy)*: No. No, actually, I don't. I was thinking, just now, that I want to call David. I want to hear his voice. But then I realized, you know, it always makes me sad. I don't think it will, and then it does.

CURTIS: Oh.

LISA: I'm gonna go visit Leonard.

CURTIS: The dying guy?

LISA: I know you think it's strange. And it's not what Mother said, at least not really. I mean, it's not a "romance." I don't think we have a future together. And it's not like when I first saw David . . . God. I looked into those eyes and they were so beautiful. Not quite brown. Not quite green. They were . . .

CURTIS: Hazel. That color is hazel.

LISA: Leonard's eyes are just plain brown. Yesterday, I was feeding him—I put some pudding on the spoon and held it to his mouth. And he looked at me, but what I saw in his eyes, his plain brown eyes . . . was happiness. It was simple. It was undiluted. Happiness. And what really surprised me—I didn't expect it, not at all—but what really surprised me, is that it made *me* happy.

(Lisa gets her purse.)

I'm going to visit Leonard.

CURTIS: Will you come back?

LISA: I don't think so.

CURTIS *(Embarrassed)*: Please? . . . I'm sort of scared.

LISA: Of what? You'll go home in a few days. Things will be just like they were. Everything will be the same.

CURTIS: Not really. Not exactly. I'll be alone.

LISA: What?

CURTIS *(Fragile)*: . . . I won't have Peter.

LISA: I don't understand.

CURTIS: He did this, to me . . . *(Starting to cry)* Peter. This man. I watched him.

LISA *(Gentle)*: Oh.

CURTIS: He did this.

LISA: I'm sorry.

CURTIS *(Quiet, to himself)*: Doesn't matter.

(She searches for something to say that will assuage her brother's pain.)

LISA: I realize that I'm no one to give advice, but maybe some day, Curtis, try people.

CURTIS: Maybe.

LISA *(Peaceful)*: I'm going to go feed pudding to Leonard. Hmmm.

(She smiles at him, then exits. We can see that Curtis feels very much alone. Despite his efforts he is crying.)

CURTIS *(To himself)*: Shit.

(After a moment, the Nurse appears in the doorway. She is chewing gum. Curtis pulls himself together.)

NURSE: They're all gone?

CURTIS: What?

NURSE *(Entering)*: Your visitors, they're gone?

CURTIS: Yes.

NURSE: Noisy group.

CURTIS: I guess so.

NURSE *(Regarding his dinner)*: Did you eat?

CURTIS: No.

NURSE: What are you trying to prove?

CURTIS: I won't eat that.

NURSE: Big man.

CURTIS: *Fuck you!!*

NURSE: Hmmm. You're in a worse mood than usual.

CURTIS: Sorry.

NURSE: Your incision?

CURTIS: No. No, it's not . . . You see a lot of things, people, right? Life, death in these rooms.

NURSE *(Running the thermometer across his forehead)*: If you say so.

CURTIS: Does it make sense to you?

NURSE: What?

CURTIS: All of it?

NURSE *(Amused)*: What? You think I can explain *life* to you? You think I'm going to have some big insight into the wreckage of your life? Shit. I'm a nurse.

CURTIS: Oh.

NURSE: All right. Here goes. The way I see it, there are no answers. Some people are happy. And some people are just lonely, mean and sad. And that's the world.

CURTIS: Oh.

NURSE: You strike me as the second kind.

CURTIS: Well, thanks.

NURSE: Don't mention it. *(Regarding his dinner)* —Should I leave that?

CURTIS: Stay a while?

NURSE: For what?

CURTIS: To talk. Just . . . talk.

NURSE *(Annoyed)*: You're not the only patient on this floor.

CURTIS: Please?

NURSE: Grow up already.

(She starts to exit.)

CURTIS: Wait! . . . One more thing.

NURSE *(Annoyed)*: What?

CURTIS *(Simple)*: . . . What's your name?

(They look at each other for a long moment. And then she decides to tell him.)

NURSE: Jeanette.

(They look at each other.)

CURTIS: Jeanette.

(He removes the lid from his dinner and takes a bite. The Nurse watches. After a moment, she walks to a chair and sits down.)

NURSE: All right, fine. What do you wanna talk about?

(He eats. Blackout.)

END OF PLAY

.

Deleted Scene

When the play premiered at the Vineyard there was an additional scene. Act Two opened with Lisa addressing the audience, in front of the act curtain. This was not in the original draft, but added later. It had been expressed to me that we didn't spend enough time with Lisa. This was my solution. I wasn't completely satisfied with the speech and so I rewrote it for the Broadway transfer. Kate Jennings Grant did a spectacular job with it! She was funny and heartbreaking and wonderful. Still, at the end of the day, it felt unnecessary. Again, I credit Kate. She created such a vivid character, so much more vivid than Lisa on the page, that we no longer needed the extra material. So after several previews we took it out. This was very painful for me, and I'm sure for Kate, although she was completely gracious about it. (She always is.) In any event, here is the speech that only a few audiences got to see:

LISA: My name is Lisa. And I'm an alcoholic.

(Recorded voices respond: "Hi, Lisa.")

I've been sober now for five years. Until Tuesday. My father's sick. I guess he's dying. I mean he is. He's dying. And the pressure just—I don't know, seeing him, at the hospital like that, I guess it shook me up. That's a lie. I mean it *was* disturbing. But that's not why I drank. We were all together—all four of us, my brother, my parents and me. And I know they love me and blah blah blah, but you can't please them. There's *no* pleasing them. And I mean really, who are they to judge me? So I had a drink? So what? You know, five years ago, when I stopped drinking, really stopped drinking, I ate *nonstop*. All day, all night. I was washing down Oreos with Big Macs. I'd tell myself, "It's not for me. I want Happy Meal toys for the kids." *Ten thousand* toys later, nothing fit and my thighs were chafing. —So, right now, to be perfectly honest, I think maybe I'd rather be a skinny drunk than fat and sober—and whose brilliant idea was it to have doughnuts at these meetings anyway? . . . Sorry, I'm sorry. Raymond, my new sponsor, is helping me see that it's not a case of either/or. I'm trying to stay cheerful—but frankly it's exhausting. David used to say— No, no. I'm not going to talk about him. David's my ex-husband and I'm trying to see him in a clearer light. I don't know why it's so hard. It's not like he was perfect. He was moody and sullen and, frankly, a little depressive. I mean his favorite movie is *Judgment at Nuremberg*!

I don't want to talk about David. The boys miss him. I mean they see him, of course, but it's not the same. So I feel like I have to pick up the slack. A couple months ago they had this thing at school, Field Day. You know, where instead of classes all the kids spend the afternoon in the yard running races and stuff. Our tax dollars at work. And Jeremy's not really very athletic. Everyone has things they're good at and things they're not. Jeremy's not athletic. Well, I went, you know, to be supportive. And he ran the ten-yard race, and the twenty-yard race and the hundred-yard. And he was last. I mean consistently last. And then this woman, one of the mothers that I'd never met, she was wearing a lot of perfume. We were outdoors and it was still too much. This other mother says to me, all smiling, she says, "Which one is your little boy?" And I don't know why I did it! I didn't think about it. I panicked. I mean I love him, I love my kids but—I pointed at some *other* kid, some *athletic* kid in a very cute top. And she asked me his name, but before I could tell her, this *other* mother taps my shoulder and chimes in with, "That's *my* son! You're pointing at my child!" And the two of them just stared at me like I was some kind of freak. They were waiting for me to explain, but I wasn't giving them the satisfaction. I just turned and left and rushed to my car. And I got out as fast as I could. I was driving very fast, so fast, in fact, I missed my street. And I thought to myself, "Just go. Just go and go and keep on going, keep driving till you're far away and no one knows you, just drive and drive and drive and drive and drive and—"

(Her cell phone rings.)

Shit. Sorry, I thought I turned that off.

(She looks at her phone.)

It's my mother. I better take it. *(Into the phone)* Hello . . . Of course.

(She hangs up. Beat. When she speaks it's as if she's been sentenced to prison.)

She wants me to pick up a magazine on my way to the hospital.

(After a brief moment of intense internal struggle, with some urgency:)

Does anyone know where there's a McDonald's?!

(Blackout.)

NICKY SILVER's plays include *Pterodactyls, Fat Men in Skirts, Raised in Captivity, Free Will & Wanton Lust, The Maiden's Prayer, The Eros Trilogy, The Food Chain, Fit to Be Tied, My Marriage to Ernest Borgnine, The Altruists, Beautiful Child, Three Changes* and *The Agony & The Agony*. Mr. Silver is the recipient of the Oppenhiemer Award, the Kesselring Prize and three nominations each for Drama Desk and Outer Critics Circle awards.